BELIEFS, VALUES, AND POLICIES

BELIEFS, VALUES AND POLICIES

Conviction Politics in a Secular Age

The Hensley Henson Lectures, 1987–1988

DUNCAN B. FORRESTER

CLARENDON PRESS · OXFORD
1989

Oxford University Press, Walton Street, Oxford OX2 6DP
Oxford New York Toronto
Delhi Bombay Calcutta Madras Karachi
Petaling Jaya Singapore Hong Kong Tokyo
Nairobi Dar es Salaam Cape Town
Melbourne Auckland
and associated companies in
Berlin Ibadan

Oxford is a trade mark of Oxford University Press

Published in the United States
by Oxford University Press, New York

British Library Cataloguing in Publication Data
Forrester, Duncan B.
Beliefs, values, and policies.
1. Christian political theology
I. Title II. Series
261.7
ISBN 0–19–826194–2
ISBN 0–19–826734–7 (Pbk.)

Library of Congress Cataloging in Publication Data
Data available

Set by Rowland Phototypesetting Ltd
Bury St Edmunds, Suffolk
Printed in Great Britain by
Biddles Ltd, Guildford & King's Lynn

For Margaret

PREFACE AND
ACKNOWLEDGEMENTS

When I was invited to deliver the Hensley Henson Lectures I felt deeply honoured, but initially hesitant, on two grounds. First, I wondered whether what I have to say might not fit easily into the remit of the lectures—'the Appeal to history as an integral part of Christian Apologetics'. Secondly, I suspected that my own position as presented in these lectures might diverge rather sharply from some of the views of Herbert Hensley Henson. Setting aside the convenient precedent of Karl Barth, who used his Gifford Lectures on Natural Theology as the occasion for a thoroughgoing repudiation of the possibility of a natural theology, I then concluded that consideration of the contemporary relationship of theology and public policy does indeed have an apologetic thrust, and necessarily involves constant appeals to the past, to history, to the tradition. For today we have to consider a widespread uncertainty about the grounding of social values and goals. In this context the Christian theologian cannot but become involved in commending the Christian faith as giving access to reality and suggesting a way of responding to Pilate's question, 'What is truth?' In short, theology may claim to provide a basis, perhaps the most adequate basis for wise and humane policy formulation. In the public realm, as in the church, its task is to bear witness to the truth.

I would love to have had the opportunity of arguing with Hensley Henson. With some of his positions I have immense sympathy. As long ago as 1924 he identified one of the themes of these lectures when he declared that there was a serious problem involved in proposing a Christian basis for 'the policy of a nation, the majority of whose citizens are in no effective sense Christian' (Suggate 1987: 36). He ventured to criticize the middle-axiom thinking that I will examine in the second chapter, and always sought, as I also do, to insist on a dogged reverence for the facts. While very properly denying that matters of social reform and public policy belong at the *top* of the Church's agenda, he showed, particularly in his attitude to the rise of Nazism, an admirable determination to root his opinions firmly in Christian fundamentals. 'Pastor Niemöller', he wrote in a letter to *The Times* denouncing Bishop Headlam's sympathy for the Nazis, 'is the embodiment of a protest which no Christian church could refrain from making without forfeiting its claim to be Christian at all' (12 August, 1938).

Herbert Hensley Henson, I believe, would find my subject at least adequately congruent with his intentions in establishing this lectureship. And I imagine that some of the things I have to say would at least have elicited from him a characteristically pungent retort.

I am deeply indebted to Professor Ernest Nicholson, Chairman of the Faculty Board of Theology, and the many others who gave me such a warm welcome to Oxford, showered me with hospitality, and discussed my ideas with such encouraging perceptiveness and charity. My friend, the Revd Patrick Irwin, arranged my stay in the congenial surroundings of Brasenose College. A number of colleagues and friends have given generously of their time to comment on drafts and outlines of this book while it was in the making. I am particularly grateful to Alastair Campbell, Robin Gill, Ian McDonald, George Wilkie, Lesslie Newbigin, Norman Shanks, Ronald Preston, and Philip West in this connection. My friend and research student, David Sinclair, has assisted with the preparation of the text for the press, and my thanks go to him. An earlier draft of part of chapter 2 appeared in *Christians and the Future of Social Democracy*, edited by Michael H. Taylor (Ormskirk and Northridge, 1982), and some paragraphs in chapter 6 come from my article in *The Scottish Churches and the Political Process Today*, edited by Alison Elliott and myself (Edinburgh, 1987).

CONTENTS

INTRODUCTION

We live in a plural society in a secular age. One would expect the influence of religion in the public realm in such a context to be vestigial. But almost the opposite appears to be the case. Not only among Islamic fundamentalists and the Moral Majority in the United States, but in countries where organized religion is in sharp decline conviction politics has had an amazing renaissance. Politicians increasingly speak in theological language, and church leaders and theologians surprisingly frequently make significant contributions to public debate. Politicians seem to need and expect religious support and theological undergirding for policies; and often the theologians see their role as questioning or even denouncing the activities of 'conviction politicians' and the effects of conviction politics. The role of theology in the contemporary public arena calls out for analysis and evaluation.

In this book I ask what service theology might render in the public realm today. What service is it capable of rendering? What are the constraints, the opportunities, and the responsibilities laid upon theology today in this regard?

And I will argue

- that theology should contribute *distinctively*, or not at all, to public policy debates;
- that withdrawal from the public arena would lead, and has indeed led, wherever such withdrawal has occurred, to a major distortion in the way Christian theology is understood and practised;
- that such a withdrawal of theology would also involve a drastic and dangerous impoverishment of public life;
- and that there is today a pressing need to re-examine the basis, content, and manner of theology's contribution in the light of rapidly changing circumstances.

In chapter 1 I explore some aspects of the modern context which deeply influence what theology is capable of doing, and suggest major theological responsibilities. I also give an indication of the general theological position from which I address the issues. Chapters 2 and 3 are primarily concerned with critical examination of two popular ways of understanding the relation of theology and public policy. Chapter 2 discusses what had become a kind of dominant ecumenical orthodoxy in this field, the so-called 'middle-axiom' method. And in chapter 3 I turn to those who see theology's primary task in relation to the public realm as sustaining cohesive social values, giving some special attention to the recent report of a working party chaired by the Archbishop of York, *Changing Britain* (BSR 1987). Chapter 4 enquires into the basis of church statements. On behalf of whom does the church speak? And is anyone listening anyway? In chapter 5 I look at some of the implications of the fact that in the public realm theology has to deal with responsible individuals, some of whom are committed Christians, and also with impersonal structures and processes. And I enquire whether the New Testament can provide useful illumination. In the final chapter, with some reference to Péguy's thought on the relation of *mystique* and *politique*, I endeavour a provisional constructive statement and summing-up.

I

THEOLOGY IN THE PUBLIC ARENA

An Arena without Rules or Referee?

We will start with a parable, borrowed from G. K. Chesterton, about a controversy in the public square, in this case concerning a lamp-post which many people desire to pull down. A monk, personifying theology, is approached for advice about ends and means, and commences, in dry, scholastic style, by going back to fundamentals, and saying, 'Let us first of all consider, my friends, the value of light. If light be itself good . . .' At this point he is rudely knocked aside, a rush is made at the lamp-post, which is down in a moment, and the people 'go around congratulating themselves on their un-medieval practicality'. That is but the start of the trouble, for 'some people have pulled down the lamp-post because they wanted the electric light; some because they wanted old iron; some because they wanted darkness because their deeds were evil. Some thought it not enough of a lamp-post; some too much; some acted because they wanted to smash municipal machinery; some because they wanted to smash something. And there is war in the night, no man knowing what he strikes.' They gradually come round to the belief that the monk should have been heeded in the beginning. Only what might have been debated by gaslight must now be discussed in the dark (Chesterton 1911: 23–4).

The parable points to a situation not unlike today's, where there are a plurality of goals and widely divergent commitments, but no agreed criteria by reference to which these conflicts may be resolved; a society whose conflicts are played out like a game of Australian Rules Football, in which (as far as I can see from watching games on television) few rules seem to be recognized, and the referees' attempts at enforcement are patchy and ineffective. We are considering here the phenomenon to which Richard Neuhaus gave the apt title, *The Naked Public Square*: politics, according to him, has been evacuated of religious and ethical substance, partly by Christianity's increasing tendency to play down its claims to proclaim *public* truth and its willingness to be confined to the domestic and individual sphere, partly by a secular, pluralist society's inability to assert agreed goals and values, a 'public philosophy', or a 'public theology'. As Neuhaus points out, a public square from which the demon of an official orthodoxy has been expelled may be swept and garnished ready for seven devils, each worse than the first, to enter in (Neuhaus 1984: 86).

A similar point has been made with increasing urgency by Alasdair MacIntyre from his early broadcast 'A Society without a Metaphysics' (1956), through *Secularization and Moral Change* (1967) to his notable *After Virtue* (1981). In 1956 MacIntyre argued that we possess an effective *morality*, which is generally accepted, and to which appeal on great moral issues is made by the contending parties. But the underlying philosophy or theology, MacIntyre suggests, has been eroded, so that we are left with liberalism in morals and politics, and nihilism in metaphysics. We may be able to jog along for a time reasonably well as long as the liberal moral consensus survives, but 'the loss of a general framework of belief engenders a loss of any overall sense of significance', and presumably in time will corrode the liberal consensus itself (MacIntyre 1956: 375). In 1967 MacIntyre added, 'The inability of men to discard Christianity is part of their inability to provide any post-Christian means of understanding their situation in the world' (MacIntyre 1967: 75). By the 1980s MacIntyre discerns that the collapse of this fragile consensus on values has already occurred. The absence of any generally accepted

metaphysic or religious position has corroded the foundations; the superstructure cannot long survive. No longer is
there any agreement about the nature of virtue or justice.
There is, he argues, now no way of resolving fundamental
intellectual disputes, such as that between Nozick and Rawls
about the nature of justice. Both claim to be proceeding
according to purely rational considerations, without appeal-
ing to fundamental axioms or assumptions about the nature of
things. But there is, according to MacIntyre, no referee who
can arbitrate between them, no way of resolving the conflict.
The claim that there are *rational* principles, independent of a
metaphysic or a theology, capable of resolving conflicts between groups with competing interests has shown itself to be
empty. There are in fact competing and contradictory understandings of rationality and of justice, resting on fiduciary
foundations which are now rarely examined and whose importance and indeed existence is frequently denied (MacIntyre
1988: 1–11, 799).

The problem as diagnosed by MacIntyre is not simply an
academic concern. The lack of a genuine moral consensus
rooted in a public theology or a public philosophy, he argues,
has devastating consequences for society. Community no
longer rests on a moral basis, with agreed goals and assumptions. The consequence is that 'modern politics is civil war
carried on by other means' (MacIntyre 1981: 236), for the ties
that bind people together at the deepest level have frayed so as
to become ineffective, and society is no more than a collection
of competing interest groups. In such an arena without rules or
referee, power is seized by the strong and used at the expense of
the weak. Policy may express an ideology ('The dominant
ideas are the ideas of the dominant class') but is no longer
constrained by a coherent and widely accepted metaphysic or
theology with an associated system of values. The barbarians,
MacIntyre concludes, have taken over; indeed 'they have
already been governing us for quite some time' (MacIntyre
1981: 245).

MacIntyre, Neuhaus, and others paint a dramatic, indeed an apocalyptic, picture which many find compelling. But even those who cannot accept their full analysis of the contemporary predicament must acknowledge that they point to real and pressing problems. There are today few shared assumptions in the public realm. Much political debate has become a battle to the death between rival dogmas which only too blatantly attempt to clothe and disguise sectional short-term interests. The assumptions that persist are rarely believed to have a necessary relationship to the Christian faith, or indeed to any general world-view, particularly one that is capable of transcending and questioning interests, that resists being reduced to an ideological weapon in social conflict. As a consequence, Christianity no longer has a privileged position in public discourse. Christian theology, like Chesterton's monk, comes to the public square not as a referee or arbitrator, not as a recognized authority to which appeal may be made, but as a participant or contributor that must demonstrate by skill and insight the value of the contribution. It does not have a reserved place in the public arena, but must constantly *earn* its position, while refusing to be recruited into the role of legitimating any secular ideology.

Three Spheres

In order to clarify the areas with which we are primarily concerned it is useful to distinguish three spheres in social life, and say something about the relation between them.

First, there is the private and domestic sphere, the space for the exercise of private virtue. Standards and values in this sphere are still often expressed in Christian terms, and there is a common recognition that religion has a function here, or even that this is the place where religion *belongs*. Since the Enlightenment it has been increasingly commonly held that church pronouncements on individual morality, family life, the media, are entirely appropriate and indeed expected, even if religion is no longer regarded as part of 'public truth' or entitled to contribute to other areas of public debate.

Theologians have in recent years expended so much energy in denouncing the increasing captivity of religion in the private sphere that they have often failed to notice the apparently increasing significance of what goes on there. People in mounting numbers appear to find fulfilment and meaning not in work or in public life but at home, in leisure activities, in hobbies and face-to-face relationships, in the family and small, more 'manageable' communities. Work is necessary to earn pay in order that 'real life' may be lived and enjoyed in the private sphere. The place of institutional religion even in the private sphere may for many people be somewhat problematical today, but there is evidence of a common assumption that religion 'belongs' in this sphere, and theology is expected to address issues arising here.

Critiques of the 'domestication' of Christianity make important points. A Christianity which has accommodated itself to the private realm lacks prophetic edge, and tends to imply a tolerance or justification of the values of the society. It inculcates 'traditional values' and accepted standards of personal morality, attitudes, and patterns of behaviour which are important for the smooth running of the system. But on the other hand, to quote J. B. Metz, 'It does not protest against or oppose in any way the definitions of reality, meaning or truth, for example, that are accepted by the middle class society of exchange and success. It gives greater height and depth to what already applies even without it (Metz 1980: 45).

But let there be no doubt about it, the private sphere is important, and increasingly important. Religion does indeed belong there, but it has an important contribution to make in other areas as well. Although this book is not primarily concerned with issues arising in the private and domestic realm, I would wish to affirm what traditional Roman Catholic moral theology calls the principle of 'subsidiarity'—that there are goods which can only be achieved within the family or small local communities and social institutions, which accordingly deserve to be encouraged and supported in their autonomous fulfilment of tasks which can far less adequately be undertaken by centralized bureaucracies or other large-scale social institutions.

The second sphere is the ceremonial, ritual, symbolic, or rhetorical side of the life of the nation—what Bagehot spoke of as 'the dignified part of the constitution'. Here the stress is upon the affirmation of national identity and the legitimation of the power structures of society and their operations. Consider in this connection the rituals marking great national and civic occasions—Remembrance Sunday, the Coronation, state funerals, royal weddings, services to mark the opening of the courts, the activities of the Queen and other members of the royal family, and so forth. 'The monarchy,' wrote Bagehot, 'by its religious sanction now confirms all our political order; it acts as a disguise' (Bagehot 1888: 43, 54). The rituals of civil religion perform much the same function in the public realm as the rituals of folk religion in the private sphere. In societies which officially reject religion, such as the Soviet Union, it becomes necessary to provide secular counterparts to the civil rituals of religion (Lane 1981). But in Christian or post-Christian societies the only profound symbolic language to hand is that of Christian faith. Hence it is frequently assumed without much consideration that Christian symbols and Christian rhetoric are inherently confirmatory of power, and that they can easily be recruited into the role of legitimation.

It is probably wrong to exaggerate the importance of Christian civil ritual today, or to argue (as David Holloway does) that the coronation service shows that Britain is still 'positively Christian', that the values of the nation are Christian, and that the church is still at the heart of things and represents or crystallizes national culture (Holloway 1987: 41–5). None the less we seem to be in a period when there is a new and often intensely felt need for religious legitimation in the public realm. Ministers and other politicians, particularly of the Right, *expect* church support, and are hurt and angry when it is denied them. A contemporary conservative theorist, Roger Scruton, sees religion (by which he understands Christianity) as reinforcing the attachment of the citizen to the forms of civil life, and the binding principle of all social institutions (Scruton 1980: 172). All this lays a grave responsibility upon Christian theology, which may be summarized as how to fulfil the function of a civil religion while retaining Christian integrity, how to crystallize and support all that is good while simultaneously addressing a prophetic word to the nation. We will return to some of these issues in chapter 3.

But the main focus of our attention in this book will be on the third sphere, which is the realm of politics and economics, where the processes and structures of the market and the polity regularly claim a greater or lesser degree of autonomy from ethical and religious control. This is a sphere apparently dominated by material interests and instrumental rationality. For centuries efforts to monitor and influence theologically what goes on in this sphere have been increasingly ineffective and lacking in trenchancy. The sphere regularly claims to be self-sufficient and self-regulating so that any outside intervention is bound to be a disturbance to the smooth running of the system. And some theological positions—most notably the neo-Lutheran—allow almost total autonomy and independence from external scrutiny to this secular sphere. But other theological traditions—and an increasing number of Lutherans as well—are today striving to work out the most effective and constructive ways of contributing to the resolution of problems that arise in this central area of social life, where great matters which profoundly affect human flourishing are at issue.

Three Understandings of Theology

We also find three general understandings of the scope and responsibilities of theology in the modern world, and of its bearing on the three spheres discussed above.

There is, first, an individualistic and private theology, which understands Christian faith as a private option without public relevance. This popular view of the nature of theology is the easiest for our pluralistic society and culture to relate to. In practice it is highly conservative, legitimating by failing to question the existing ordering of things. It is, in effect, the civil theology of post-Enlightenment bourgeois society, having successfully assimilated the values and assumptions of that society. Its domain is 'religion' (as commonly understood in the modern world), subjectivity, and the so-called 'spiritual realm'.

There is certainly, as we have suggested earlier, a place for a private theology, in the sense of a theology which considers issues arising in the domestic and personal sphere. The problem is that modern theology has only too often allowed itself to be limited to engaging with such matters, and withdrawn from the public realm, as in existentialist theology in its various forms, with its exclusive preoccupation with subjectivity, 'authentic existence', and I–Thou relationships. Such emphases easily confirm the modern assumption that theology has nothing to do with public, inspectable truth, in the dual sense of truth that is accessible to all, not the arbitrary option of a minority of 'cognitive deviants' (Berger 1970: 19–42), and truth that engages with issues on the public agenda.

The second view sees theology as one academic discipline among others, with its own clearly demarcated field. Like the first type of theology, it regards itself as having a bearing on a restricted part of life, and recognizes clear limits to its competence and its enquiries. It belongs in the academy, and outside may, or may not, recognize some responsibilities towards the church. In relation to most matters on the secular agenda it can say nothing, precisely because it is an academic or churchly discipline with its own clear frontiers. While this position reflects very clearly the intellectual fragmentation of modern academic life, many of its protagonists follow a paradoxical course of first proclaiming the limited competence of theology and theologians, and then themselves making pronouncements far beyond the limits they have imposed.

For example, Professor Gordon Dunstan in an article on 'Theological Method in the Deterrence Debate' defines theology as 'an intellectual discipline . . . possessing an integrity and autonomy of its own in that it handles a corpus or body of material of its own in a disciplined way . . . in its nature, an application of reason to the things of God, primarily the self-revelation of God' (Dunstan 1982: 46). Accordingly he announces that many matters cannot be discussed in Christian or theological terms at all: 'There is no specifically "Christian" way of waging war, or of amputating limbs, or of fixing oil prices, or of deciding for or against the nuclear generation of energy' (Dunstan 1982: 40). On such matters it follows that the theologian can have nothing to say *qua* theologian. But this does not appear to impede Professor Dunstan, as a Christian theologian, from discussing with great shrewdness and insight issues in medical and business ethics, and declaring in the same article that something called 'Christian realism' (presumably a way of doing theology) teaches 'the duty to deploy and control effective power', including the nuclear deterrent (Dunstan 1982: 49–51; cf. West 1986).

On what grounds may such theologians venture beyond their self-declared professional competence? Dunstan and others suggest that theology may provide a kind of backdrop for the drama of public life which highlights the significance of what is happening 'on stage'; that theology and the Christian faith imprint a character on those who carry responsibility, helping them to act with prudence and integrity; that theology may provide a pious preface and a consoling conclusion to a secular discussion. And, most important of all, the resultant theology teaches a general acquiescence in the structure of things and the exercise of authority. Dunstan claims to derive his results from a broad consideration of the New Testament. A contemporary Dutch Calvinist theologian, H. M. Kuitert, reaches very similar conclusions but bases them rather on a Durkheimian account of the nature and function of religion, to which Christianity and Christian theology must apparently conform (Kuitert 1986).

Theologians who argue in this way usually fall back on some version of Luther's 'Two Kingdoms' theory, which is also capable of providing a kind of explanation of their conservatism. But they are not consistent in that they engage in certain kinds of theological foray into the secular world, and discountenance others, for reasons which seem to be more ideological than theological. And their narrow view of the scope and responsibilities of theology finds precious little in the mainstream of Christian theology to support it. A private or narrowly academic understanding of theology is a distinctively modern misunderstanding.

The third way of understanding theology and its responsibilities asserts that theology is in principle concerned with the wholeness of life as a consequence of belief in the universal lordship of Jesus Christ. Theology may have something to say about anything, but it does not necessarily have a word about everything. It certainly will not tolerate being confined within that part of life labelled in the modern world 'religion', nor is it limited to a spiritual realm so that it has nothing to say to temporal concerns. It is not confined to the sphere of human inwardness and subjectivity.

The greatest modern exponent of this kind of theology was Karl Barth, and it is not without cause that Kuitert, in defending his narrow and academic understanding of the scope and nature of theology, blames Barth for sowing the seed that has sprouted into the liberation theology of today. Barth was emphatic that theology cannot with integrity avoid operating in the public realm. But for him, as for the liberation theologians, it has a *distinctive* contribution which it must make in public debate. It comes to the public square *as theology*, not simply and exclusively as ethics. Barth calls for, and himself provides, not watered-down theology, but rigorous, challenging, disturbing theology, calling for transformation, repentance, and a new order—the kind of theology which is itself a way of proclaiming the gospel and being obedient to Jesus Christ.

This view imposes on the public interventions of theology limits of a very different sort from those suggested by Dunstan or Kuitert. For Barth and his like, theology adopts a kind of self-denying ordinance so that 'no more be said in addressing the urgent political problems of the present day than can clearly be said on the basis of Christian truth and insights' (Ramsey 1969: 30). For the rest, theology must keep silent. Public issues may sometimes be addressed obliquely rather than directly, by doing one's theology with ever greater seriousness and application. Barth, for instance, argued that his most substantial contribution to the liberation of Germany from Nazism was the writing of the numerous hefty volumes of the *Church Dogmatics*, in order to reaffirm and revive authentic Christian dogmatics (Barth 1969: p. xi)! A sense of timing is also important: it is too late to denounce genocide when one is standing at the gates of Auschwitz. And it is a waste of breath to add theology's voice to what everyone else is saying anyway. A high degree of responsibility is required if theology is not to cry 'Wolf!' so often that nobody pays any attention. And it is pointless to speak out regardless of whether anyone is listening.

The Changing Public Role of the Church

A theology which is capable of addressing issues of public policy has perforce to be a *church* theology. It is not a free-floating theory or a detached ideology. It is rooted not just in a community of scholars but in a believing fellowship which, while it may transcend space and time, has a *face* (or rather, faces) in our land. This fellowship is also a community of moral discourse which, among other things, concerns itself with social values, goals, and norms. Theology, however, is more than the mouthpiece of the church or of its magisterium, proclaiming and elucidating the outcome of ecclesiastical deliberations. It has a clear responsibility both to take part in discussion within the church, and to contribute to public debate even when it cannot do so as an authorized mouthpiece for the institutional church. Fidelity to the gospel can sometimes be in tension with the current teaching of the institutional church, but not with a deeper loyalty to the church of Jesus Christ. There is, or ought to be, a critical solidarity between church and theology.

The decline in the numbers and influence of the church has important consequences for theology. In such a situation much academic theology keeps quiet and 'minds its own business', defining that business in rather narrow terms. When challenged as to its relevance it asserts that it is investigating 'objectively' a religious tradition which has shaped western culture profoundly. As an academic subject, so the argument runs, theology belongs alongside classics or ancient history. It treats Christianity as largely a human phenomenon to be studied in a detached way; on principle it declines to engage with the truth claims of Christian faith or investigate faith from the inside. At the other extreme, theology may retreat into becoming a narrowly churchly study, allowing the internal housekeeping and struggle for survival of a beleaguered institution to set its agenda. In neither case is theology seen as engaging with a fundamental, but increasingly neglected, dimension of contemporary public truth.

Theology has to be, in a sense, the conscience of the church, reminding it that it is more than an institution among others, implicated in a society and a culture, and often reinforcing and reflecting that society's tensions and problems. It must help to restrain the panic of a declining church by reminding it of perennial responsibilities, and challenge the timidity and reluctance to change so characteristic of small and ageing congregations by insistent reminders that the significance of the church as an institution is entirely derived from the Kingdom which it proclaims and the nature of which it is intended to exemplify in a partial, but nevertheless real, fashion.

When the church becomes a less and less significant functioning part of the social system a church theology has to face distinctive dangers—of irrelevance, of ignorance of the facts of the case, of a utopianism unconstrained by awareness of the ambiguities and limitations of the situation. But it is also possible that the church may in such a situation be set free to *be* the church rather than fulfilling the role of 'religion' in the social system. And this also presents responsibilities and opportunities for the recovery of theological authenticity. At such a time Paul Ramsey's call becomes even more pressing: 'There is urgent need, and now is the time, for those of us who love the Church, and who share in striving for an ecumenical ethics in the world of today, to engage in a probing examination of what we are doing (and consequently failing to do) in formulating the Church's address to the world' (Ramsay 1969: 19–20).

It is that examination on which we are now embarking.

2

PRINCIPLES AND POLICIES

In this chapter we will examine the argument that the main contribution of theology to public debate is neither in the indicative mood—an interpretation or analysis of what is going on—nor in the imperative mood—the authoritative pronouncement of specific directives. It is rather, so the argument runs, in the derivation from Christian premises of indications of the general direction that policy should follow in a specific situation that the value of theology shows itself most clearly. Theology, in other words, is centrally concerned with the movement from the indicative to the imperative, with motivation as well as understanding. Theology and ethics must never be separated. The task, accordingly, is to lay down principles, both general principles of a more or less universal validity, and intermediate principles which are relevant and operational in a particular context. But it is rarely if ever possible or appropriate, it is argued, for theology to advocate specific policies or a particular course of action. These intermediate principles have often been given the somewhat misleading name of 'middle axioms'.

What may be called the 'middle-axiom approach' was formulated in the 1930s and was initially most closely associated with that quiet but immensely influential ecumenical statesman, J. H. Oldham. Oldham's approach was followed very closely by William Temple, John Baillie, J. C. Bennett, and a host of others, and middle axioms became the accepted currency of ecumenical social ethics for a generation. More recently the middle-axiom approach has fallen out of favour, for reasons we shall examine, but strenuous efforts are being made to reconstruct and commend this approach in social ethics by R. H. Preston, G. R. Dunstan, Dennis McCann, Alan

Suggate, and others (Preston 1983, app. 2; 1981, chap. 3; Dunstan 1974, esp. chap. 3; McCann 1981; Suggate 1987).

The middle-axiom method encompasses, as we shall see, a *procedure* in ecumenical social ethics (which we argue should be affirmed, with some important modifications) and a *logic* of the proper relationship of theology and public policy (which we will question).

Procedure

The middle-axiom approach has always, and properly, emphasized that theology is too important a matter to be left to the theologians. Accordingly the appropriate way of doing ecumenical social ethics, of developing a Christian approach to matters of public policy, is to gather together groups of people with varied and relevant skills and experience to ana-lyse the matter in hand, engage with the facts of the case, reflect theologically, and make recommendations. Such groups always include 'experts', and people with practical experience of the problem as well as theologians. It is important, argues Oldham, to include people with the responsibility for taking decisions because 'seen from the inside a problem has many aspects that are concealed from an outside view' (Oldham and t'Hooft 1937: 219). The task of the group is to establish the facts and the constraints of the situation and understand how these are analysed in the secular world. Only then should it attempt a Christian judgement upon them. In the fulfilment of this task theologians work alongside other Christians—a useful reminder that theology is a participative affair. Above all, it is felt important that theology should relate to the constraints and possibilities of the situation and avoid vacuous and high-flown generalities which do not impinge helpfully upon the policy options which are available.

Interdisciplinary group work is surely to be welcomed. It has produced a whole string of important contributions to social ethics (Preston 1981: 95). In a small way at least, interdisciplinarity involves an overcoming of the fragmentation of modern intellectual life, allowing a more rounded view of a problem. Competitiveness, boundary-maintenance, and misunderstanding between disciplines have harmful results. Important questions which lie in a kind of no man's land between specialities may be neglected, and other issues which require the simultaneous illumination of various disciplines may be left in the dark. Interdisciplinarity involves tearing down barriers of suspicion and competition to enable a fuller encounter with the truth in its wholeness. It is thus a search for the recovery of an unfragmented vision, not unrelated to the destruction of the dividing wall of hostility which Ephesians 2 sees as a consequence of the cross of Christ.

These 'Oldham groups' are also almost invariably ecumenical. This involves a recognition that it is no longer plausible to attempt to sustain or revive confessional systems of social ethics. Older efforts to propound an Anglican, a Calvinist, or a Lutheran ethics are not viable today. Even Roman Catholic moral theology has come to have remarkably little in method or approach to distinguish it from Christian ethics in general, although Vatican pronouncements on ethical issues continue to rely on rather old-fashioned styles of natural-law reasoning. It is as if the various traditions are now contributing to a common enterprise. Furthermore, the older ecumenism, dominated by white Protestants from the northern hemisphere, has now given way to the far broader and more variegated ecumenism of today. This introduces new and difficult tensions into ecumenical ethics. But these tensions are certainly healthy, helping social ethics to grow out of eurocentrism towards a greater universality and a wider scope and relevance.

What is the role of theology, the contribution of the theologian, in such interdisciplinary groups? In the past it was sometimes easy for the theologians in an Oldham group to become little more than the initial enablers and the final mouthpieces of the group, modestly reflecting the group's opinions, attitudes, and conclusions. Such is not, of course, theology at all; it is simply the articulation of the informed opinions of educated people of good will, and it lies wide open to the charge preferred by E. R. Norman and others, that it is nothing but the conventional values of the intelligentsia, decked out rather unconvincingly as Christian theology, which are being presented. At its worst, such theology becomes no more than a mouthpiece for the power élite.

But fortunately there have been those who, while rejecting the idea of the theologian as a solo performer, and affirming the value of wide participation in the forming of Christian opinion on social issues have had a special concern for the theological *proprium*, the distinctive contribution of theology to the discussion. Ian Ramsey, for instance, who was himself deeply involved in a series of groups which produced notable reports, affirmed

the need for a classical theology which gives us the necessary professional background, and also for what has been called a 'contextual' theology where believers develop the facility for latching onto the multiple discussion of a problem. Such a discussion not only aims at a creative decision; in reaching such a decision it discovers also new possibilities of theological articulation. It is in this contextual theology that there will be found the growing points of our faith and the intimations of a new culture, a culture Christian, scientific, technological and humane (in Edwards 1973: 38).

This call for a dual theological input, the 'classical' and the 'contextual' needs to be carefully heeded; it suggests that the theological *proprium* is dangerously distorted if either component is omitted, or if the balance between them is wrong. Only if the theologian has a care for a proper and distinctive contribution to the discussion, indeed suggests a framework within which the discussion may take place, will the results go beyond being well-informed and genial, and become in some sense an expression of the Christian gospel.

Oldham groups have traditionally brought together theologians, secular experts (usually academics), and decision-
makers, from politics, industry, or the professions. The role of
the experts is to guide the analysis and interpretation of the
facts. The decision-makers know the problems from the inside
in one sense—they are aware that the room for manœuvre is
limited, that compromise is usually necessary, and that the
options on offer are likely to a greater or lesser extent to be
morally ambiguous. These perspectives are of the greatest
importance, particularly for curbing any naïve idealism by
'earthing' the discussion in the realities of the situation.

But theologians, experts, and decision-makers come from
the ranks of the powerful and the privileged. Their knowledge,
and their social, educational, political, and ecclesiastical situation together give them an influence and control over resources
which make them part of the 'power élite'. They take decisions
which affect the lives of others in all sorts of ways. Even in a
democracy it is often unclear in what sense they are account-
able for their decisions to those affected. Experts, civil
servants, and ecclesiastics also have their interests, their
prejudices, and their blind spots—particularly perhaps the
frequent inability to understand their own limitations. Experts
have interests in common which tend to make them sympathetic to one another and sometimes strangely insensitive to the
needs and problems of people whose life-experience is very
different. Experts are not the eagle-eyed, dispassionate, and
altruistic Guardians dreamed up by Plato in the *Republic*, who
know the Good, and therefore what is good for others as well
as for themselves. They are rather men and women, with skills
and insights which are of great importance, but occupying a
place in society which can limit their insight and empathy, and
subtly distort their values.

That is why it is so important to involve as full participants
in the discussion those who are poor and powerless, the people
who are more the recipients than the makers of policy. These
are the people who know where the shoe pinches. But it is not

easy to involve them in the discussion, to allow them to speak, and to take with a proper seriousness what they say. They are often angry, muddled, and naïve. They rarely have the capacity for rigorous, disciplined thought which higher education is intended to nurture. They not infrequently have a very narrow and materialist vision, and have difficulty in appreciating the constraints and the considerations which dominate the minds of the powerful. They, too, are sinners. But from the point of view of Christian theology their situation and their life-experience, their reactions and their distinctive insights make them indispensable contributors to the discussion. They balance and challenge the prejudices and the limited insights and the selfishness of the powerful. And the tensions and the disturbance which they bring can prove immensely fruitful if they are empowered to have their say, and are attended to with modesty and seriousness. Their voice must be heard.

The introduction into the discussion of those previously excluded certainly makes it more difficult, in the short run at least, to reach a common mind. They bring with them experience, insights, and attitudes which are not easy to accommodate in a group of powerful and influential people. The Oldham approach assumed rather facilely that agreement on a Christian position of a general sort should not be too hard to reach. When achieved, it expected that it would be something with which most 'decent folk', people of good will, or 'men of prudence' would concur.

Even when the powerless are not included in the discussion, it appears now to be considerably more difficult to reach agreement than once it was. To give two recent instances: The British Council of Churches Working Party on Poverty chaired by Professor Raymond Plant, failed to reach enough of a common mind to produce an agreed report (Moyser 1985: 328–9; BCC 1982). About the same time a Church of England Board for Social Responsibility group charged with making a Christian evaluation of economic theories could do no more than produce a booklet of essays representing a range of different points of view (BSR 1984). The Oldham approach appeared to work when there was a greater degree of consensus among the élite than there is now. The collapse of consensus, which we discussed in the first chapter, raises acute problems for the Oldham method, which seemed unaware that it rested upon such fragile foundations. The church is not exempt from the modern cultural crisis. The new intellectual polarization is felt in the church as well as in society, and is especially serious when the church's discourse is conducted in a secular idiom, or when theology acts as no more than a veneer for an ideological argument.

Logic

The 'Oldham group' approach to the doing of social ethics is very valuable, provided the composition of the groups avoids an élitism which excludes all but 'experts', provided the facts of the case are confronted and analysed seriously, and provided special care is taken to ensure that there is a well thought out theological contribution.

But the group method in itself does not tell us much about the nature and logic of middle-axiom reasoning. For this we cannot do better than go back to J. H. Oldham's account in the preparatory volume for the Oxford Conference on Church, Community, and State, *The Church and its Function in Society*. Oldham writes:

The Gospel is not a code of morals or a new law. But the new mind which is formed in those who have responded to the revelation of a new reality in Christ must express itself in new forms of behaviour. It belongs to the prophetic and teaching office of the Church to expound the implications of the Christian understanding of life and to make clear the kind of behaviour to which belief in the gospel prompts.

Such broad assertions as that Christians are bound to obey the law of love or to strive for social justice do not go far towards helping the individual to know what he ought to do in concrete situations. To give him precise instructions to be literally carried out is to rob him of his moral responsibility as a person. It is not the function of the clergy to tell the laity how to act in public affairs, but to confront them with the Christian demand and to encourage them to discover its application for themselves. Hence between purely general statements of the ethical demands of the Gospel and the decisions that have to be made in concrete situations there is need for what may be described as middle axioms. It is these that give relevance and point to the Christian ethic. They are an attempt to define the directions in which, in a particular state of society, Christian faith must express itself. They are not binding for all time, but are provisional definitions of the type of behaviour required of Christians at a given period and in given circumstances. (Oldham and t'Hooft 1973: 209–10)

Middle axioms, in John C. Bennett's words, 'are not absolute and all-inclusive goals, but the next steps that our generation must take. The Kingdom of God in its fullness lies beyond our best achievements in the world but God does have purposes for us which can be realised' (Bennett 1954: 81). They are, according to the Amsterdam Assembly of the World Council of Churches, 'those goals for society which are more specific than universal Christian principles and less specific than concrete institutions or programmes for action' (WCC 1948: 158 n.)

Oldham, Bennett, Temple, and John Baillie believed that mediation is necessary: basic Christian principles must be filtered through middle axioms or the like before they can be put to work by the political decision-makers. The middle-axiom approach affirms both the relevance of Christian faith to public issues and also its transcendence over any particular policies.

Examples of middle axioms were cited by Temple in the seventh chapter of *Christianity and the Social Order* (1942). These concerned the family, the sanctity of the individual, and the principle of fellowship:

(*a*) Every family should be decently housed.

(*b*) Every child should have the opportunity of a good education, which encourages full development, is inspired by faith in God, and finds its focus in worship.

(*c*) Every citizen should have a secure income enabling the maintenance of a home and the proper rearing of children.

(*d*) Every citizen should have a say in the conduct of the business in which he works.

(*e*) Every citizen should have adequate leisure.

(*f*) There should be liberty of speech, assembly and association. (Temple, 1942: 73–4)

Temple and the other proponents of the middle-axiom approach hoped that most, if not all, Christians—and many others as well—would be able to agree on such goals. But disagreement becomes inevitable, they believed, as soon as we turn our attention to the question of implementing such objectives.

Middle-axiom thinking thus involves four stages or levels. The first is the basis for the whole operation. It is the Christian faith, understood in a very general way. What is involved here is something like 'the essence of Christianity', what all Christians have in common, or the deposit of faith, rather than any denominational or confessional, and therefore divisive, development or interpretation of the faith. This is seen as the foundation on which all—or most—Christians may agree and on which they may base co-operation across sectarian and theological differences. As Oldham put it: 'The basis of the Christian ethic is faith in a living, personal God who has disclosed His grace and His will in Jesus Christ. The gift and the promise are prior to any ethical demand' (Oldham and t'Hooft 1937: 235).

From this is derived the next stage: fundamental ethical principles which are authentically Christian because they are implied in the formulations of stage one, but which none the less may be widely shared by many non-Christians. These are principles of great generality, and affirm such things as human dignity, together with social structures such as the family and the nation, within which human beings may achieve their destiny. As William Temple sums up: 'Freedom, Fellowship, Service—these are the three principles of Christian social order, derived from the still more fundamental Christian postulates that Man is a child of God and is destined for a life of eternal fellowship with Him' (Temple 1942: 54).

Thirdly, between these general statements of principle and ultimate ends, derived from the gospel and concrete decisions, choices, and policies, come the middle axioms. Middle axioms link together principles and action; without their mediation one cannot proceed from ethics to implementation. They cannot be formulated by the theologians alone because they demand a careful analysis of the context and of the situation. In other words, theology and empirical analysis must come together in the formulation of middle axioms.

When we come to the final stage—implementation—we have moved well beyond the professional competence of the theologian, who must now leave to lay people to work out how to put Christian principles and middle axioms into practice. The derivation of policies and practices from middle axioms is in fact the most contentious stage of the process. Temple, Oldham, and others believe this stage must be left to individual Christians rather than the church. It is seldom legitimate or proper for the church as an institution to endorse a particular policy or programme. Middle axioms, it must be recognized, may be implemented in a variety of ways. It is prudent to make these choices in the light of the best expertise available, but inevitably there will be disagreements among Christians about the application of Christian principles. 'It is not the church's business', writes Paul Ramsey, 'to recommend but only to clarify the grounds upon which the statesman must put forth his own particular decree. Christian political ethics cannot say what should or must be done but only what may be done.

It can only try to make sure that false doctrine does not unnecessarily trammel policy choices or preclude decisions which might better shape and govern events' (Ramsey 1969: 152).

The middle-axiom approach commended itself very widely for forty years or more. Despite its vagueness it has a common-sensical quality. Although this is seldom acknowledged, it has close parallels in established procedures in moral theology. According to Ronald Preston it was responsible for a whole series of distinguished and influential contributions to public debate. Yet since the 1970s there has been a mood of dis-enchantment with middle axioms, for reasons that deserve attention:

(i) The procedure is clearly deductive and presupposes a particular, and rather Platonic, understanding of the nature of theology. One starts by formulating what one might call pure theological truth; from this one elicits general principles of a universal nature; from these one derives middle axioms, or statements of the bearing of general principles in a particular context, providing a sense of direction; and finally (by the least clearly defined stage in the process) one chooses among the various policy options which might implement the middle axiom. It would not be good to place against this deductive procedure only an inductive alternative, suggesting that one starts from quandaries and problems in the public realm and works back to a fresh understanding of the Christian faith. But that would probably be preferable to seeing the public arena as the place where Christian dogmas and principles, indepen-dently arrived at, are to be applied in an almost mechanical way. The doing of theology cannot be insulated from the life of the world and its problems without making theology extra-ordinarily abstract, so that it becomes increasingly difficult to relate it in any constructive way to these problems and quan-daries. The liberation theologians have reminded us that there is no such thing as 'pure theology', fashioned in the academy and uninfluenced by its context or the interests of its formulators and guardians; there is no innocent theology. Living theology, they correctly affirm, moves constantly between engagement in the life of the church and the world, and the interpretation of the Christian revelation. All true theology bears the marks of this involvement and of these interests. And the faith, the commitment, the engagement, is prior to the theology. It is therefore not true, as Paul Ramsey suggests, that in politics the church and theology 'are only theoreticians' (Ramsey 1969: 152); they are necessarily also participants, and only on the basis of their involvement are they capable of theorizing.

(ii) This deductive process involves the highly controverted movement from the indicative to the imperative mood. We need not enter into the great debate about the relation of the 'is' and the 'ought', save for some cautionary remarks about the way in which middle-axiom thinkers move between the two. Middle-axiom thinking appears to presuppose a liberal theological position of a Ritschlian sort. Religion in this way of thinking is seen as essentially about value. A sharp distinction, almost as emphatic as that of Max Weber, is drawn between fact and value. The theologian accordingly is seen as an expert on matters of value, whose competence does not extend to matters of fact. These last are seen as the domain of social science, which is assumed to be value-free. The gulf between fact and value can only be bridged in a fragile and temporary way by co-operative endeavour between theologians and social scientists working from opposite sides of the chasm. These assumptions about the nature of theology and social science and about the relation of fact and value are, of course, highly contentious and would be rejected by many if not most theologians and social scientists today (Elliott 1978: 175–6).

An alternative approach stresses the primary importance for Christians of 'is' statements. These are at least as significant as normative or value statements. John Habgood puts the point well when he writes:

The prime Christian contribution to social ethics is in the indicative rather than the imperative mood . . . It is Christian belief about the kind of place the world is, about the depth of human sinfulness and the possibilities of divine grace, about judgement and hope, incarnation and salvation, God's concern for all and his care for each, about human freedom and divine purpose—it is beliefs such as these which make the difference, and provide the context within which the intractable realities of social and political life can be tackled with wisdom and integrity. (Habgood 1983: 168)

But the argument needs to be pushed further. These indicatives can best be seen coming together in a story, rather than a theoretical system, a story which is the irreducible core of the Christian faith. Any great tradition, as Alasdair MacIntyre shows, rests upon a canon which is largely in narrative form —Homer and the Bible, to name but the two most obvious examples (MacIntyre 1988: 11). Dogmas, principles, and ethical systems are time-bound endeavours to give an account of the significance of the story in terms of a particular culture and age. It would be fatal to demythologize the story, to reduce it to doctrine or directives, and then cast the story aside as redundant and unhelpful, its meaning and importance exhausted in the particular interpretation. The story is what ultimately matters, and *this* story is evocative: it grabs us and grafts our story into itself. It cannot be told or heard without an awareness that a response is called for. There is an ethic contained already within the story, a challenge and a disturbance.

In a real sense, then, it is telling the story with all its inner vitality and depth of meaning which is the truest Christian contribution to the public realm. And from this point of view the attempt to distil from the story Christian principles, so that Christianity may thus, and only thus, have a bearing on the situation is misleading. As Lesslie Newbigin points out, our modern European culture predisposes us to see the story as illustrative of principles or of dogma, in such a way that when we have grasped the principles the story may be jettisoned.

Principles, he reminds us, can easily become demonic, whereas an authentic sense of the source and goal of the human story relativizes such timeless principles as justice, freedom, and human rights (Newbigin 1981: 349–61). It is the story rather than the principle which helps us to interpret the signs of the times and find their meaning. It is the story which gives guidance. This conviction has been developed in the exciting 'narrative ethics' of James McClendon and Stanley Hauerwas (McClendon 1986; Hauerwas 1983).

But how can a *story* shape *policy*? Karen Lebacqz suggests an answer to this question. Justice as it was understood by the Israelites, she argues, flows from the story of the people: 'Justice is grounded in *remembrance*.' The laws which outline the nature of justice are set in contexts which constantly remind the people of their history. It is this, the shared experience of the people of God, their common story, the community identity which gives meaning and content to their understanding of justice. They have come to know what justice is through their dealings with the just God, just as the early Christians were enjoined to 'Love each other *as I have loved you*' (John 15: 12). Only through the experience and the memory do we know what love and justice are; the story also enables us to love and to do justice: 'We love *because he first loved us*' (John 4: 19). Thus, she continues

The grounding of Christian justice in remembrance puts a premium on *story-telling*. If the story is not told, justice will die. The refrain 'I am the LORD your God' must retain meaning for the community. It retains its meaning only if the story out of which it comes and from which it gains its meaning continues to be 'alive' for the people. This means that worship and preaching—the re-enactment of the story in 'memorializing celebration'—are integral to justice, they keep alive the story that grounds the identity of the community in its history of justice and injustice (Lebacqz 1986a: 2–4).

Thus the story of God's justice and the experience or memory of this God's dealings with his people precede and define our

understanding of justice and our endeavours to act justly and
secure structures of justice.

A similar position is developed in fascinating detail in
Alasdair MacIntyre's *Whose Justice? Which Rationality?*
(1988). He argues that the major intellectual projects of
Christian thought were endeavours to produce systematic
philosophical and moral reflections which were consciously
rooted in, and inseparable from, the Christian story. The idea
of an autonomous theoretical and moral structure, purely
rational and not grounded in a tradition and a story, was
almost inconceivable until modern times. And the fact that the
link between the story and understandings of justice and of
rationality has for most people been cut is at the root of our
modern predicament (MacIntyre 1988).

To put the point about the relation of story and principles in
another way: the narrative *contains* the imperative. Or, in Karl
Barth's terms, dogmatics (understood as ordered reflection on
the Christian story) can be viewed *as* ethics, and any independent ethics, or indeed ethics which claims to be derived from
dogmatics, is to be viewed with great suspicion. Accordingly I
find it strange that John Habgood can write in the middle of
the fine passage about the distinctive Christian indicatives
which was quoted above, these words: 'In terms of the principles by which people should live and societies order
themselves, Christians have little to say that could not be said
by any reasonable person of good will' (Habgood 1983: 168).
If the story is distinctive there must surely also be something
distinctive in the response it evokes—and in the ordering of the
life of the community that proclaims and lives by that story. If
the story, the Christian 'indicatives', do not challenge or
disturb in any way the knowledge and the norms that reasonable people of goodwill possess in any case, the story is
dispensable. It may and should be set aside so that 'reasonable
people of goodwill' may co-operate on the basis of a shared
ethic and a common rationality.

It is precisely the filtering out of distinctiveness which is one of the central flaws in middle-axiom thinking. The principles and middle axioms are said to be derived from the Christian faith, but share little, if anything, of the specificity, distinctiveness, or offence of that faith. They are assimilated without difficulty by 'any reasonable person of good will'. Theology simply adds its voice to the roar of the decent majority.

This point was raised interestingly at the First Assembly of the World Council of Churches at Amsterdam in 1948. A Dutch government official, Dr Patijn, objected to the promulgation of general principles as the proper expression of the contribution of the churches in judging social question.

Whence come these general principles to be proclaimed? [he asked]. From human wisdom, from the natural law, from theological constructions like the orders of creation and corporate groups, from a *mélange* of liberal philosophy and the unacknowledged intrusion of national aspirations and class interests? Under the guise of general principles the pretensions of human wisdom obscure the light of revealed truth and biblical counsel, disassociated from its concrete significance expressed in concrete circumstances, is transformed into a dead language using the adages of worldly wisdom (Duff 1956: 108).

In rejecting abstract and general statements as the churches' contribution Dr Patijn called for a stand to be taken on specific burning issues if the churches' prophetic responsibility was to be fulfilled (Duff 1956: 106; WCC 1948: 155–75).

Nor do principles, whether general principles or middle axioms, necessarily provide the most appropriate Christian guidance to responsible decision-makers. 'Our deepest perplexity', wrote Dr Patijn, 'is that the problems of society are for the most part of such a technical character that there is little or no apparent relation between many decisions to be taken and the driving ethical principles of the Christian faith' (WCC 1948: 159). Technical problems require technical solutions, and norms, or the personal character of the decision-makers are less important by far than the responsible person's knowledge and skill. But the church must not allow itself to be intimidated by the suggestion that its judgements are invalidated by the largely technical nature of the problems: at every point ethical and religious considerations are interwoven with technical factors, and the church has a responsibility to judge and assess the issues at stake in the light of the gospel. Dr Patijn concludes:

It is useless in such cases to proclaim theories about the true natural order for economic or international life since no one in real difficulty will get help from mere abstractions. To remind a godless society in its burning points of conflict of its responsibilities, will only have effect if the full weight of prophetic judgement is thrown into the balance at the heart of the real difficulties and at the right moment, with the greatest possible knowledge of the facts (WCC 1948: 161).

Goals, principles, middle axioms may be important, but they are only part of the Christian gospel's contribution to the handling of problems in the public realm.

So we return to the question of distinctiveness. John Habgood appears to believe that in social ethics Christianity has hardly anything to say which is not perfectly acceptable to most rational people of good will. In other words, it is platitudinous. 'The price of agreement in such general statements is', according to Raymond Plant 'vacuity' (Moyser 1985: 321). It is better to stand with R. H. Tawney (who never identified himself with middle-axiom thinking) who, when asked whether Christianity had anything distinctive to say about the way people ought to act towards their neighbours, replied that if it has the leaders of the churches ought 'whatever the cost, to state fearlessly and in unmistakable terms what precisely they conceive that distinctive contribution to be. If they do not, then let them cease reiterating secondhand platitudes, which disgust sincere men, and bring Christianity into contempt' (quoted in Oldham and t'Hooft 1937: 213–14). This is a challenge to which we shall return in the next chapter.

Finally, it is necessary to question the sharpness of the separation between middle axioms and policies. Middle axioms, as their proponents ceaselessly argue, give a sense of direction, but are not specific directives. The church may affirm middle axioms, but must stand back from advocating particular policies, because that is a contentious matter beyond the church's competence. Policy choices must be left to laymen and to experts. But principles and middle axioms cannot be understood, elucidated, or assessed except in relation to the policies which might be used to implement them. Principles need to be tested, reconsidered, and modified in the light of the experience of trying to make them operational. Yet middle-axiom thinking strenuously suggests that any problems which may arise must be the result of bad implementation; the principle itself is immune to this kind of criticism. Experience does not lead to reconsideration of principles. But it is really impossible to expound or defend or criticize principles without considering how they work out in practice. As R. H. Tawney said, 'to state a principle without its application is irresponsible and unintelligible' (Tawney 1953: 178).

Policy choices involve technical considerations in which theologians and church leaders have no special competence, and taking sides on political matters easily threatens the unity of the church and the fulfilment of its pastoral functions —these are the kind of considerations which persuaded cautious ecclesiastics that the church should seldom if ever become more specific than proclaiming middle axioms. But this kind of caution—which certainly has its proper place —can verge on the irresponsible if it is made a more or less binding guide-line. It is surely highly significant that the two most important and influential Church of England reports in recent years—*The Church and the Bomb* (BSR 1982) and *Faith in the City* (Archbishop's Commission on UPAs 1985) both advisedly set aside the middle-axiom logic and make specific policy proposals, thereby inevitably 'taking sides' in political debate. Had they not done so, and contented themselves with analysing the situation and enunciating principles or middle axioms one may suspect that they would have aroused far less interest and made less impact than they did (Elford in Moyser 1985: 185 ff.). If an object of church reports is to affect 'the way things go' and influence public debate, these two documents have been far more efficacious than any other recent contribution which stops short of making policy recommendations.

The middle-axiom method seemed to work tolerably well while Britain was a much more outwardly Christian country than it is today, during the time when there was a considerably higher degree of social and political as well as religious consensus. But even then in times of crisis it seemed to provide little if any help in 'discerning the signs of the times' and responding to them appropriately. The conflicts and tensions of the period of the General Strike do not appear to have been illumined by middle axioms, and indeed the reluctance of churchmen thirled to the method to go beyond generalities muted the Christian witness. Middle axioms did not enable leading churchmen to see through the Munich Agreement or warn of the dangers of appeasement. William Temple and others were not compelled by middle axioms to denounce area bombing and massive direct attacks on the German civilian population; Bishop Bell of Chichester was a lone voice among church leaders (Hastings 1986: 191, 348, 377). Besides, key social, ecclesiastical, and theological assumptions of the method are no longer available. We now need to look for a way of contributing to public debate which no longer takes it for granted that Britain is a Christian society. And those who take seriously the ideological predicament of the West may legitimately enquire whether Christian theology has anything distinctive and constructive to offer in times of crisis as in more settled periods.

The classical middle-axiom thinkers tended to take goals, ideals, visions more or less for granted and concentrated most of their attention on providing middle-level and immediately relevant guidance to decision-makers. In the next chapter we turn to discuss those who see theology's contribution as having little to do with directives or imperatives which relate to contemporary problems, but rather as concerned with the sustaining of values, visions, and general long-term goals for society.

3
CHANGING BRITAIN? VALUES AND VISIONS

In the previous chapter we examined an influential method, called rather loosely the 'middle-axiom' approach, whereby it was believed that Christian theology may give general guidance and a sense of direction to those grappling with specific decisions and options in the public realm. This method involved bringing together 'Christian principles' distilled from theological premisses, and an empirical analysis of the situation in order to assist decision-makers in their choices and in the formulation of policy. We saw that middle-axiom thinkers characteristically draw a sharp frontier, which theology may not cross, between the general guidance that theology may offer, and specific policy choices. Theology provides a sense of direction rather than directives. For theology to specify and require a specific course of action is for it to go beyond its remit and its competence. The proper people to take such decisions are the responsible policy-makers and politicians acting, one may hope, in the light of the general guidance offered by theology.

Middle-axiom thinking sees theology's contribution as largely concerned with *principles*, with general rules of action, with the orientation of behaviour, and with the formation of character. The procedure as a whole is focused primarily upon policy choices. In this chapter we turn to those who believe that theology is concerned not so much with specific ethical conundrums faced by the policy-makers, as with the injection, or implantation and nurturing of Christian *values* in public life. Theology, in other words, has the task of engaging with the underlying assumptions of a society and a culture about the nature of human beings, about human flourishing, about human destiny and human fellowship, about the relation of the social order and a transcendent order (if such is believed to exist), about the way a community allocates worth and chooses its goals. These are the sort of 'values, expressed or unexpressed', which in the Archbishop of York's words, 'underlie all moral and political action' (BSR 1987a, p. i).

There is an argument which can be traced back long before Max Weber to the effect that most of the values of Western society, even if they appear today transposed into an entirely secular form, are nevertheless in origin derived from the Judaeo-Christian tradition, which down the centuries has powerfully shaped the values and assumptions of Western culture so that today most of these values in their secular dress seem self-evident or 'rational'. Theories that there is a connection between Christian values and assumptions and the origins of modern science and the rise of capitalism are familiar. In the quite recent past they were not infrequently used apologetically: if Christianity was capable of generating such excellent developments, there must indeed be 'something in it' which deserves further consideration, and possibly intellectual acceptance. Such arguments have now been stood on their head: if Christian values lead to ecological disasters, nuclear warfare, the ruthless exploitation of human beings and of the natural environment, and mounting injustice, we had better be atheists or devotees of some less aggressive Eastern faith.

This discussion is important, but it could easily tempt us away from the matter in hand to more general themes. It has been necessary to make three points. First, Christianity (like other forms of religion) has, as a matter of historical fact, fed values and assumptions into our society and culture through worship, preaching, education, and prophecy. Max Weber provides an illustration in the course of a comparison of Indian and occidental society. He suggests that the resolution in favour of eucharistic and general commensalism of the debate in the early Church about whether Jewish and Gentile

Christians should eat together was not simply a matter of tremendous importance for the first Christians. It profoundly shaped the western conception of community, and of the proper form of human relations.

The elimination of all ritual barriers of birth for the community of the eucharists, as realised in Antioch, was, in connection with the religious preconditions, the hour of conception for the occidental 'citizenry'. This is the case even though its birth occurred more than a thousand years later in the revolutionary *conjurationes* of the medieval cities. For without commensalism—in Christian terms, without the Lord's Supper—no oathbound fraternity and no medieval urban citizenry would have been possible (Weber 1958: 37–8).

While much of this process of the implantation of values is entirely unconscious, the Christian church has regularly, and properly, seen part of its role as the sustaining and refreshment of Christian values in society. Secondly, it is not at all easy to distinguish what in our value system is derived from Christian sources and what comes from elsewhere. Values may emerge from various and sharply differing sources, and the same values may be held and affirmed by people of contrasting fundamental convictions, and justified and explained in various and contradictory ways. To mention just one not untypical case: the value of equality has Judaeo-Christian roots, and Stoic roots as well. The two sources generate rather different emphases and give the concept of equality different content. But in the operative value of equality the two strands are closely and inextricably intertwined. In the third place, values that are of religious—in our case Christian— provenance may easily become detached from their roots, so that the fact of their historical link with Christian faith becomes a matter of indifference, or of merely academic interest, to most of those who espouse the value. Religious people often worry whether Christian values can survive when the tap-root nourishing them from the soil of faith is cut. But most secular people, if they concern themselves with these matters at all, think rather of an umbilical cord which must be severed if the infant is to flourish and mature.

Those in contemporary Britain who see theology as having a major responsibility for the implanting and nurturing of Christian values divide into two sharply contrasting groups. In the first group are people who see theology's task as sustaining and supporting consensual and natural values which are already widely diffused in our culture, and are necessary if society is to cohere and be healthy. These values may in origin be, for the most part, Christian, but it is held that they may now be commended and defended in a secular, rational, or naturalistic fashion. This position is effectively presented by the Archbishop of York in his book *Church and Nation in a Secular Age* (Habgood 1983), and more recently in the Report of a Working Party of the Church of England Board for Social Responsibility which Dr Habgood chaired, entitled *Changing Britain: Social Diversity and Moral Unity* (BSR 1987a).

The second group consists of those who see the Christian faith, and Christian values and visions in particular, as being sharply at variance with the conventional values of our society. Their view of Christianity is that it enters in as a challenging, disturbing, and questioning element, often in protest against the dominant values, often confronting easy consensus, refusing to accommodate itself to the assumptions of twentieth-century industrial capitalism, or to act as a civil religion, legitimating and authorizing the existing value system. People who might be put in this category include Bishop Lesslie Newbigin (Newbigin 1983, 1986), Charles Elliott (1987), and Alasdair MacIntyre—in particular the fascinating conclusion of his *After Virtue* (MacIntyre 1981).

The position of the first group rests upon certain key assumptions which require critical examination.

The first assumption is that Britain is a highly integrated society which, despite the steady decline in Christian observance and the new religious pluralism, continues on the whole to subscribe to 'Christian values'. *Changing Britain* relies heavily on the evidence presented in *Values and Social Change in Britain* (Abrams *et al.* 1985) to support this assumption. This study reported that 'the British are to be seen and see themselves as a relatively unchurched, nationalistic, optimistic, satisfied, conservative and moralistic people' (p. 12). As compared with the countries of southern Europe, Britain is found to be, along with the other north European countries, more secular. But it is in a class of its own in the ardent advocacy of 'Christian values'; 'They [the British] are in their normal geographical-cum-cultural position with respect to the religious Commandments to worship only one God, not to take His name in vain, and to keep the Sabbath. But with respect to honouring their parents and the injunctions against murder, adultery, theft, envy and lust they out-do the Scandinavians, Northern Europeans and Latins in virtuous declaration' (Halsey in Abrams *et al.* 1985: 12). Not only are these values particularly widely affirmed in Britain, but the British are seen as singularly optimistic, patriotic, and reluctant to question authority. Accordingly, *Changing Britain* starts with the assertion that Britain is 'in world terms, an old, stable, large and successful culture' (BSR 1987a: 1). That apparently is the context within which change is to be considered.

Britain, then, is seen as still dominated by Christian values and still at heart a Christian culture, despite secularization and despite the increasing numerical strength, and vitality, of other religions. But in the present depleted state of the church it is necessary to look for allies in sustaining Christian values. John Habgood, for instance, looks with some expectation towards folk religion, in the belief that Richard Hoggart was right that in England folk religion combines suspicion of overt religiousness with a stress on decency and a basic morality, which Habgood apparently identifies with Christian values (Habgood 1983: 79). But he is well aware that what have been called 'the confused syncretisms of folk religion' (Williams

1985: 21) are sometimes in tension with the church and its teaching, and that it would be risky to claim that the Church of England is an expression, or an unqualified supporter, of the folk religion of the English people. He at least notes the view of Visser t'Hooft and others that folk religion is neo-paganism, an alternative to Christianity rather than the bearer of Christian insights and Christian values. But Visser t'Hooft had experienced at first hand how Nazism had claimed to be the folk religion of the German people and had set itself, with much success, to subvert the Christian Church (Habgood 1983: 83). This, however, does not shake John Habgood's confidence in English folk religion as a support of the central Christian values.

Nor is it, according to *Changing Britain* simply the widely diffused and persistent folk religion which can be the bearer of Christian values in a secular age. In the weakness of the churches, other religions also may be looked to for help in sustaining fundamental Christian values. Professor Halsey, in the Values Study, argues that the other great religions now present in Britain in increasing numbers

abound in commonalities: the centrality of prayer to religious practice, the significance of individual life as a balance of virtue and vice determining a future beyond death, the insignificance of individual life in the pages of eternity, the rootedness of religious belief in family continuity and the ultimate belief in one God. This last seems capable of translation into a common ethical creed of love, hope and charity binding a nation and extending towards all mankind, even all creation (Abrams *et al.* 1985: 16).

It is, perhaps a reassuring vision: despite appearances, Britain remains a Christian society. Christian values and Christian assumptions are deeply rooted in our culture. Christian moral insights are such as to commend themselves spontaneously to all decent people of goodwill. And in sustaining these values, it is suggested, the church finds powerful allies in folk religion and in the other world faiths, which share the same values, while seldom labelling them as Christian.

It may be a comforting picture, but is it not a bland and inaccurate portrayal of the moral and religious confusion of British society, while the ominous coalition of tribal folk religion and Christian faith in Northern Ireland continues to kill people? And is its starting point not the axiom that there is no place for that which is distinctive, perhaps even abrasive, in Christian morality? Conventional values of decency and conformity, after all, led to the Cross.

The second assumption of *Changing Britain* is that cultural assimilation on the part of church and theology is to be welcomed as an opportunity rather than a danger. There may be little that is new in this. All our churches have often followed strategies of accommodation. But usually they have not acknowledged or rejoiced in the fact. David Gerard argues in the Values Study that mainstream Anglicanism followed a strategy of accommodation rather than resistance to social forces in the nineteenth century, and in the twentieth century demands minimal commitment, 'requiring neither deviation from the generally accepted ethical and social standards of the wider society, nor burdensome donations of time, money or energy' (quoting Gilbert 1980: 112; Abrams *et al.* 1985: 75–6). Whatever the fairness of that judgement, it is at least a question whether accommodation is desirable or a dangerous dilution. But history in itself does not make accommodation desirable, or other than a dangerous dilution of the meaning and challenge of Christian faith. Something has surely gone seriously amiss if the role of theology in the public realm is no longer seen as in any sense confession of a faith which is at odds with the world, or confrontation with the powers. *Changing Britain* seems to have less to do with instigating changes or challenging changes than with constructive adaptation to developments which are taking place anyway. This is perhaps hardly surprising, since the report has sought to approach problems 'with criteria and insights which belong to the best in our society, rather than ones imposed upon it from outside' (p. 64). In other words, the possibility of words of judgement and of hope, rooted in the Christian gospel is excluded in place of what can be no other than the *Zeitgeist*. The danger here is of a form of 'culture Christianity' which is incapable of questioning the values of the society in which it is placed.

The third assumption follows from this reduction of Christian values to 'criteria and insights which belong to the best in our society': Christian values, or what is left of them, must now be presented in a naturalistic or rational way. Detached from their Christian roots they can now quite easily be commended to decent men and women, who instinctively affirm them anyway. Most people agree about basic morality; it is almost a matter of indifference what one's own faith or metaphysic may be, because on the really important matters (like fair play, and decency, one supposes) most people are agreed. The working party seems totally oblivious to Alasdair MacIntyre's problematic, as discussed in chapter 1. Agreement persists, they believe, on the really significant issues, and this ethical consensus may be rooted in almost any world-view on offer. Christian ethics at most is natural ethics writ large and suffused with emotional warmth. To quote Nigel Biggar's perceptive *Latimer Comment*: 'Here the Church is permitted to speak only in confirmation, not in criticism; only to second, not to propose. The Church may proclaim more loudly the good the world already knows; but not the good that comes to the world as news' (Biggar 1987: 3).

We should not be surprised that in his shrewd 'Theological and Pastoral Reflections' on the Values Study Professor Jack Mahoney enlists the results of the survey to support his view that values are not essentially dependent on religion (Abrams *et al.* 1985: 253). Once again, Christian values and Christian ethics are declared to have no inherent and necessary connection with Christian faith, and to be in no really significant respect distinct from a purely secular morality of decency and prudence. Iris Murdoch has discerned a serious and distressing 'void in our thinking about moral and social problems'.

Because of 'the loss of religion as a consolation and guide . . . most people lack the words to say just what is felt to be wrong' (in Mackenzie 1958: 227–9). *Changing Britain* suggests we do not need a religious language to tell us what is right, and that theologians and Christians have no distinctive responsibility to give a Christian account of what is wrong.

The fourth assumption of *Changing Britain* is the crucial one: the Christian church is the guardian, purveyor, and exemplar of the values that hold society together; its function is to provide social cohesion; and fortunately, in an integrated and stable society like Britain there is a high degree of consensus about values, which the Christian church should accordingly confirm. Shared moral values are 'the stabilizing principle for a society' (p. 22). Theology's role appears to be this: it should concentrate on strengthening social cohesion and confirming shared values rather than seeking to contribute to the resolution of conundrums and conflicts. And certainly the task is not to add to the questions society already faces, or to highlight and publicize tensions. The Church of England —and other churches as well—should continue to play the role traditionally assigned to them: to act as a unifying force, and as a source of values (p. 15).

It is as if Émile Durkheim had been invited to write our ecclesiology! Religion, according to him and other functionalist sociologists, provides a social cement and is primarily concerned with holding society together. Its role, to use the language of more recent sociology, is to provide a 'sacred canopy' under which social institutions may be secure and justified. Or, in the terminology of Talcott Parsons, religion is the crown of a social system and generates the values which sustain that society in being. As Anthony Giddens has shown, sociology also was obsessed with questions of social cohesion until the 1970s (Giddens 1987). Sarah Maitland, one of the members of the BSR Working Party, in her note of reservation, recognized quite correctly that a functionalist view of the church and of society underlay the arguments of *Changing Britain*. She went on:

> I do not think it is the duty of the Church to be 'the heart of a heartless world', to be the social glue of a society, but rather to change, to transform. From this perspective I do not feel happy putting my name to a report which does not, I feel, adequately stress the structural justice issues facing Britain today, both domestically and internationally. In particular this report is, for me, seriously inadequate in its account of class divisions, racism and sexism in our society (BSR 1987a: 70).

This is precisely what one would expect to happen when a working party consciously and explicitly eschews serious theological reflection: it falls back unconsciously on alternative dogmas, in this case, those of rather out-of-date sociology.

Two brief concluding comments on *Changing Britain* before we move on:

(*a*) The stress on values is developed in such a way as to exclude theology, and theological questioning, from the start. It is assumed not only that there is a vital natural morality, independent of the Christian revelation, to which most people suscribe, but also that this natural morality is in fact the same as Christian morality. The result is predictably bland, with little of the New Testament's reiterated insistence that God's call involves a radical and disturbing demand, and radical and disturbing questioning.

(*b*) The report is not so much concerned with transforming, or converting, Britain as with accommodation to changes which are already taking place in response to a variety of factors and developments, political, economic, and ideological. On the whole these changes are positively assessed, and in consequence they are to be welcomed rather than resisted. There is not much anger—about what unemployment does to people, about child poverty, about the conditions in which many old-age pensioners have to live, about British racism, about Northern Ireland. Nor is there sober analysis of such disturbing situations and problems. This is perhaps not surprising in an assessment of British society which appears to be almost entirely untheological as a matter of principle.

Those who see a profound, and increasing, conflict between Christian values and the dominant values of our society are not impressed by empirical evidence such as that produced by the European Value Systems Study Group. They, for their part, produce evidence of a deep alienation of Western society from the Christian faith and also from Christian values. They suggest that there is a widespread reluctance to face the implications of the epoch-making changes that have occurred and are still occurring in our ways of thought and of behaviour.

Lesslie Newbigin, for example, returns to Britain after a lifetime of work abroad as an ecumenical statesman and finds Britain a profoundly pagan country, and British Christianity 'in an advanced case of syncretism'. It can no longer distinguish the gospel message from the culture of our day, which is uncritically 'absorbed without posing a radical challenge' (Newbigin 1983: 23). Peter Berger the sociologist describes Christians as 'cognitive deviants', inevitably marginalized in a society which operates on assumptions which are quite incompatible with Christian belief. (Berger 1970: 19–42). Alasdair MacIntyre prods us to recognize that the barbarians with their values have already taken over, so that the dominant ideas of our culture are no longer Christian or humane, that for some time there has not existed the kind of consensus about decency, goodness, and fellowship on which the edifice of *Changing Britain* rests. The style of accommodation sought by *Changing Britain* costs too much. It is the attempt to blend together incompatibles.

Back in the 1920s R. H. Tawney was already arguing that theology had been driven out of the public arena, or had chosen to evacuate it, leaving in possession not a natural code of decency, prudence, and fair play, but another creed, 'a persuasive, self-confident and militant Gospel proclaiming the

absolute value of economic success' (Tawney 1921: 230).
Tawney saw this new gospel—which has in recent years
returned with renewed force and arrogance—as a false gospel,
a modern paganism fundamentally opposed to the Christian
faith and Christian values, and hence a denial of the justice of
God, involving oppression of the poor and weak and the
glorification of the rich and powerful. Hence, he argued, it
raises a strictly theological issue, and calls for a theological
response. It must be witnessed against, not dallied with.
'Compromise is as impossible', he wrote, 'between the Church
of Christ and the idolatry of wealth, which is the practical
religion of capitalist societies, as it was between the Church
and the state idolatries of the Roman empire' (Tawney 1926:
280).

Still others see not so much consensus or contradiction as
confusion about values in our society and culture. We no
longer know what human flourishing may be. We have lost
any kind of coherent system of shared values on which a
healthy community life may rest. According to MacIntyre the
lack of such a basis inevitably threatens our society, and it
becomes urgently necessary to discover, or rather to rediscover, sustainable forms of community. We must experiment
and think, and above all await the coming of 'another—doubt-
less very different—St Benedict' (MacIntyre 1981: 227, 245).

Michael Ignatieff, in his remarkable book, *The Needs of
Strangers* (1984) concurs. Consistent moral behaviour, he
argues, requires some minimum degree of agreement as to the
preconditions of human flourishing. Yet it is just this that we
lack today: 'A decent and humane society requires a shared
language of the good' (Ignatieff 1984: 12, 14). But we have
instead in our secular culture a 'generalised silence . . . about
the whole category of man's spiritual needs' (Ignatieff 1984:
99). Our culture and its dominant values simply dodge questions of ultimate meaning. But the need for meaning is a fundamental human and social requirement: 'We can no longer
offer each other the possibility of metaphysical belonging:

a shared place, sustained by faith, in a divine universe. All our belonging now is social' (Ignatieff 1984: 78). Others, such as Jeremy Seabrook, sound a similar note of wistfulness and alarm. Something vital has been lost in the process of secularization, something that impedes our flourishing and our true sociability or conviviality, to say nothing of our salvation.

All these thinkers cumulatively suggest the inadequacy, and indeed danger, of the approach of *Changing Britain*. More is required of theology in relation to values than to affirm and interpret, and by implication justify, the dominant values of the day. The assimilation of Christianity to any culture endangers Christian distinctiveness and authenticity. But that is not to suggest that Christian theology can or should see the task as the restoration of an acceptable and coherent social cosmos under a sacred canopy. Theology cannot produce a new system of values like a rabbit out of a hat. Whether it likes it or not theology is deeply implicated in culture and society. If there is a crisis in our culture, theology shares in it fully, and bears its marks in itself. Yet theology must never allow itself to become totally assimilated to culture; it must struggle to be free. We have to wait, and we have to be faithful, and we have to confess that the truth is to be found in Jesus Christ.

In seeking a renewal of values, in waiting expectantly for the coming of a new St Benedict, in challenging rather than confirming the conventional values of our society, we are seeking to confess the faith and make that contribution which only Christianity can offer. All down the centuries Christianity has generated and sustained values, but this has for the most part been done as a by-product or spin-off from the endeavour to proclaim the gospel and live the life of the Kingdom. When theology sees its role as sustaining and affirming the dominant values of any society it tends to degenerate into a legitimating ideology, the ally and weapon of established social forces, a culture-Christianity which potentially has all the problems of the culture-Christianity of Germany in the 1930s.

In the next chapter we look at the question of the basis for theology's contribution to debates about policy, and ask in whose interests theology speaks, to whom the word is addressed, and whether anyone is listening in any case.

4
SPEAK OUT! FOR WHOM?
TO WHOM?

Why should the Church Speak?

A bishop should 'speak out', the church should say something
—how often have we heard such calls, particularly in times of
crisis and controversy, and particularly from people and
groups who are seeking support for their own position on
some contentious issue. And bishops, moderators, synods, and
assemblies *do* speak out, perhaps only too frequently, on an
amazingly wide range of issues. One sometimes wonders
whether the majority of these statements have any impact at
all.

In this chapter we will discuss the basis for church statements—why church leaders and synods have this compulsion
to pronounce on public affairs, and why so many people
outside the churches expect the churches to speak out, at least
on certain issues. We will then enquire for whom the church
speaks, whose interests it has in view. And finally we will ask to
whom church statements are addressed, and enquire whether
anyone is listening after all.

Stalin's famous question—'How many divisions does the
Pope have?'—is reiterated in varying form by people, some of
whom are sympathetic and others hostile, who regard the
church as one significant institution among others in society,
and therefore entitled to a voice in public affairs. In this view
the church is not a voice crying in the wilderness, but remains a
significant part of political society. Its views, like those of the
Confederation of British Industries, the Trades Union
Congress, and the Women's Royal Voluntary Service, should
be attended to whenever the subject matter is appropriate. The

churches are still commonly believed to have a right to be heard, and a responsibility to speak out clearly on issues such as abortion, marriage law, or AIDS, for example. Inquiries and royal commissions on subjects such as experiments on human embryos, surrogacy, or organ transplants are quite likely to include a theologian in their membership, presumably because these issues most obviously involve considerations about the nature and destiny of human beings, and theologians are seen as custodians of a great and relevant tradition of moral discourse.

Yet society's, or government's, assessment of where the church should be given a say does not necessarily agree with the church's own understanding of its responsibilities and competence. John Selwyn Gummer, when Chairman of the Conservative Party, declared that bishops can no more pontificate on economics than the Pope could correct Galileo on physics (*Guardian* 29 Apr. 1985). Instead, he sees the church as having 'a vital pastoral role in guiding the politician in the exercise of his profession . . . but it cannot give me the answers to political questions'. The leadership of the church, on the other hand, sees its pastoral responsibilities and its faithfulness to the gospel as compelling it to point to the effects on people and on communities of economic policies, and believes it must give attention to examining the presuppositions and values of economic theories. It would, in short, be impossible for the church to allow a government, political party, or pressure group—or even society as a whole, for that matter—to dictate the limits of its competence and prohibit it from speaking on anything else. It is quite proper for the present Home Secretary, Douglas Hurd, to criticize the churches' 'sometimes bizarre choice of priorities for discussion' (*Guardian* 6 Feb. 1988), but it would be quite another thing to attempt to impose an agenda on the churches. And it would be irresponsible to forget that in a pluralistic democracy all sorts of groups are eager to recruit churchly support. Their wooing can sometimes be seductive.

Our question, 'Why should the Church speak?', focuses attention on the church as a social institution, and one of the more problematic institutions today, clearly in the throes of prolonged decline in numbers and in influence. Many see it as more or less moribund, thrashing around like a stranded whale. Or, because it is a relic, an anachronistic irrelevance. One would have thought that numerical decline inevitably meant that less attention would be paid to the church, that its statements would have less significance. Surprisingly, the opposite seems to be the case today, with the depleted churches having a higher profile in the public arena than they have had for many decades, perhaps because politics has become more doctrinaire with the emergence of the New Right and the collapse of consensus, perhaps because the weakness of many other institutions has forced the churches into a more frequent questioning of government policy.

Declining churches have a strong tendency, we are told, to be timidly conservative. There is much to suggest that this is so among the British churches, particularly in the pews. Timid Christians find that the only issues on the public agenda on which they happily and successfully mobilize are matters like the amendment of the abortion legislation and the rejection of the Sunday Trading Bill, the defeat of which was hailed by some as a major triumph, demonstrating that Britain is still a Christian country (Holloway 1987: 15–22). Such whistling in the dark should convince no one. And in any case it suggests an extraordinary narrowing of Christian social concern.

Churches, like all social institutions, have an in-built tendency to defend their own interests, to fight their corner, to speak for their own constituency. The problem for the Christian church is how to speak and act in the public arena *as* the church, how to proclaim the Kingdom rather than defend the interests of an institution, how to show that it is other than one social institution among many, but the sign and foretaste of the Kingdom of God. The Church should speak out, that means, when it believes it has a mandate from God to do so, when it is constrained to speak not by the need to defend its own life, but by the gospel.

The *Kairos Document* produced by a courageous group of South African theologians and church leaders in 1985 provides an important critique of theology which is shaped by concern to protect the standing and harmony of the institutional church. We should heed the warnings in this document. The Kairos theologians see what they call 'Church theology' as uncritically and repeatedly proclaiming a few stock ideas derived from the Christian tradition without seeking to earth them in contemporary reality by way of serious social analysis and the strenuous endeavour to 'read the signs of the times'. In effect church theology proclaims a cheap grace, reconciliation without repentance, peace before justice. The oppressors and the oppressed are expected to be nice to one another without the conflicts of interest between them being faced or resolved. Church theology nails its colours bravely to the fence, and is so determined to be even-handed that it never says anything clearly. It rests on a quite unbiblical type of faith and spirituality, which emphasizes individual conversion and passive waiting upon God. It addresses its questions and its challenges and its comments almost always to the powerful, to the state or, in the case of South Africa, to the white minority community. A strong hidden motivation for such church theology is to avoid bitter internal conflicts within the church and to enhance its credibility and standing with the powerful. These motives are in themselves, of course, not despicable. But if they bulk too large not only is the church's public witness blunted, but the church itself is deprived of an opportunity to engage with the gospel. The church makes statements, but they are in general terms, and cost nothing. To give an example from closer to home: everyone, virtually, in the British churches publicly expresses opposition to racism—although the sociologists have produced disturbing evidence that in the pews there are concentrations of racism, and of anti-semitism as well (Gill 1988: 9–10). But when profession of high ideals is suggested to have practical implications—like contributing to the Special Fund of the Programme to Combat Racism, or campaigning against an immigration bill—a huge proportion of Christian people draw back. It is easy to come down in favour of goodness, decency, and peace as long as it costs nothing. Besides, a very large proportion of British Christians do not believe that there is widespread and deep-seated racism in British society. They need to attend to the experience of their black fellow-citizens and fellow-believers (*Kairos Document*, 2nd edn 1985: 9–16).

The church should speak out, whatever the cost, when constrained to do so by the gospel. It speaks to announce the Kingdom, to proclaim the gospel, to affirm the justice of God, not to defend its own institutional interests.

For Whom does the Church Speak?

(*a*) We have seen that it is inherently problematic when the church speaks for itself, particularly when it sees this as the main or sole reason for intervention in the public arena. Problematic it may be, but surely it is legitimate for the church to claim the space to live and the freedom to proclaim the gospel? Yes, indeed. But even these should not come at the top of the church's priorities. We should learn from the experience of the German Confessing Church in the 1930s which resisted Nazi attempts to control the church and claimed autonomy in its own sphere, narrowly defined, long before it recognized the holocaust of the Jews and others as *the* great issue for the Christian conscience and the Christian faith. The freedom which the church of Jesus Christ may claim for herself must not be so circumscribed and turned in upon itself that it becomes impossible for the church to *be* the church. Indeed the church claims freedom in order to be able to speak on behalf of others, and address its message to all. In claiming freedom for itself the church claims freedom for all.

(*b*) There is, however, a sense in which the church as it is now, an institution deeply implicated in our society, fragmented, compromised, and often unfaithful is called to speak for the true church, the bride of Christ, without spot or wrinkle or any such defect, the great church, or the coming church. This is part of what it means for the church to speak *as* the church and *for* the church. One dimension of this is that church leaders and synods are today aware in a way few of them were in the past that they really belong in the world church, that already in a real but partial sense the ecumenical church exists.

Some of the implications of this may most easily be illustrated by the example of the US Catholic Bishops' Pastoral Letters on war and peace and on the economy (US Catholic Bishops 1983, 1986). Here the bishops, very properly, and like the leaders of any other Christian denomination in the United States, are addressing primarily American issues and American responsibilities. They instigated a prolonged period of consultation, encouraging the widest possible debate on their successive drafts. They made extensive use of the views of experts. They consulted the faithful, and others as well. They sought to exercise their teaching office in continuity with the tradition, and to ground their thinking in scripture and in theology. Although they were concerned with the American context and related their ethical work to their own geographical sphere of pastoral responsibility, they felt that it was not enough to root things in Christian soil. There must be some co-ordination with what other hierarchies and churches were saying on similar issues. In dealing primarily with US problems and responsibilities, the hierarchy sought to represent the one church. Although there is no reason why churches in different contexts must say the same thing, there *is* a problem if the hierarchies of France and Germany take, as they did, a very different line from the Americans on deterrence. The Vatican has clearly been exercised both about national hierarchies arrogating substantial teaching authority, and about the resultant divergencies. We do not have space here to discuss adequately these two superb documents. That they were developed in dialogue, and sometimes controversy, with the Vatican and with several other national hierarchies shows that Rome is becoming a new kind of world-wide forum for Christian ethical reflection and moral discourse.

The interventions in the public realm and the contributions to debates on social ethics of the Church of England—or of any other denomination, for that matter—are today closely observed and frequently commented upon by Christians around the globe. The new ecumenical arena of the World Council of Churches is not a centralized authority like Rome. Its discussions are often tempestuous, but frequently force us to take on board new considerations, and make us realize that even as simple an action as buying a packet of tea in Oxford or Edinburgh may involve us in responsibility for poverty in Sri Lanka or Bangladesh, or be a symbolic act of not inconsiderable importance. The development of the ecumenical movement in the last thirty years and its emergence from domination by white Europeans and North Americans has exposed the churches of the wealthy and prosperous countries to the anger and the fears of their fellows in the poorer countries, and in particular to their sense of grievance and exploitation. It is no longer possible for any church to look at its own issues of public policy in isolation, unaware that when a tea merchant sneezes in London, crowds of people catch a cold in Bangladesh, or neglectful of the fact that the public utterances and activities of any church are today scrutinized and assessed by other churches around the world. All feel implicated in the actions and statements of each. In relation to the churches' stances in public affairs there is a new realization of the truth and significance of John Donne's famous statement:

The Church is Catholike, universal, so are all her Actions; All that she does, belongs to *all*, when she baptizes a child, that action concerns mee; for that child is thereby connected to that Head which is my Head too, and engraffed into that *body*, whereof I am a *member*. And when she buries a Man, that action concerns me; All mankind is of one *Author*, and is one *volume*. (Donne 1945)

The ecumenical movement has contributed powerfully towards an authentic sense of fellowship within the body of Christ and solidarity in the human family. This is the great new fact in the churches' orientation towards the public realm.

But the structures and procedures of the ecumenical movement are far from being beyond criticism. Its procedures have been attacked with some justice even by sympathizers such as Paul Ramsey (Ramsey 1969: 124–8). In reaction particularly against the World Council of Churches Conference in Geneva on Church and Society (1966), which marked a sharply radical move and underlined the marginalizing of Western church leaders and academics in this area of the WCC's work, Ramsey drew a comparison between papal and World Council statements, much to the advantage of the former. *Pacem in Terris*, he said, is 'a model of the Church speaking relevantly to the world without ceasing to be the *Church* speaking. Its merit is that it avoids becoming an exercise in specific policy making. The merit is also that by taking care *not* to speak too specifically to the world, the church was not led away from its primary task of speaking the whole of the Christian understanding of man's political existence . . . By remembering to speak for the church, it spoke more fully for man' (Ramsey 1969: 126). That is well said. But it also requires to be recognized that a lot of men and women do not find statements of such generality as speaking for them, or addressing their condition. They look for some word that is more specific and concrete. There are still multitudes of problems about how to relate the measured theological statements that are intended to give guidance in a variety of situations and the responses to particular crises and problems which take full account of the experiences, emotions, and sufferings involved. The ecumenical movement is today constraining us to move beyond the older ways of contributing to the public realm without, one hopes, losing the notable insights that that work produced.

The fundamental problem with Ramsey's position is that he suggests that the church should always speak in generalities. But the church's Lord speaks, calls, and commands in concrete and specific fashion. Moses, standing at the bush that burned but was not consumed, was not like a knight at his initiation, enjoined to defend the right and protect maidens in distress. Rather, he was addressed and commanded in a quite specific way: God has heard the cry of his oppressed people and seen the bitterness of their bondage. Therefore God sends Moses back to Egypt, back to the court, to demand of Pharaoh that he let God's people go. God's word comes as a concrete challenge. It is the same today. That modern martyr, Archbishop Romero, affirmed that the preferential option for the poor is incompatible with a 'false universality which always ends in a complicity with the powerful'. 'We see clearly', he continues, 'that there is no possible neutrality: we place ourselves at the service of the life of Salvadorians, or we are accomplices in their death' (Mahoney 1987: 334). Generalities are not enough. We must respond to the specific situation in which we find ourselves, and relate to the real neighbour, and challenge the actual oppressor.

The ecumenical movement provides a unique forum in which church interventions, which in no way rise above the national interest, are shown up as threadbare and inadequately Christian, and which encourages convergence in the general ethical stance. And in as far as the church is capable of demonstrating that it is being healed, that reconciliation is taking place within the church, it is enabled to speak with more authority of reconciliation and peace in its address to the world. The church as it seeks its fuller unity is looking forward with increasing eagerness and commitment to the life of the coming Kingdom.

(*c*) In the third place, is it the role of the church to speak *for the nation*? In Scotland, for instance, there has been a persistent tendency in recent decades to claim that the Church of Scotland in some sense *represents* Scotland, and that in default of a separate legislature the General Assembly of the Church of Scotland functions as a kind of parliament. When in 1969 the Church of Scotland gave evidence to the Kilbrandon Commission on the constitution its representatives justified their appearance before the Commission on the grounds that although the church *qua* church has no expertise in constitution making, as the 'national Church ministering to the Scottish people in every parish, the Church of Scotland is deeply concerned for the welfare of the Scottish nation' and is 'widely representative of public opinion in Scotland, more so than any other body in Scotland at the present time' (*Crowther–Kilbrandon Commission* 1969: 40, 52). As W. B. Johnston points out, we have here 'a different premiss from that of the Declaratory Articles which speak of the Christian faith of the Scottish people. The ground of credibility is not that of a church expressing the corporate faith of a nation, but a geographical claim to be a body with its agents and institutions placed in every part of Scotland' (Elliot and Forrester 1986: 6). On this basis, and disregarding the fact that it is now absurd to identify the Church of Scotland with the church in Scotland, and that Scotland is much less of a Christian country than it used to be, the conclusion is drawn that the Church of Scotland is the most representative institution in the nation, and may thus speak for the nation. Such claims are less credible now than once they were. But even if a church did in fact encompass the majority of people in a nation, is representing the nation, and expressing national feeling, a proper function for the church of Jesus Christ? Is the task not rather to proclaim the gospel to the nation, or in terms of the noble *Articles Declaratory of the Constitution of the Church of Scotland in Matters Spiritual* of 1921 to 'represent the Christian Faith of the Scottish people' and 'maintain its historical testimony to the duty of the nation acting in its corporate capacity to render homage to God, to acknowledge the Lord Jesus Christ to be

King over the nations, to obey his laws, to reverence his ordinance, to honour his Church and to promote in all appropriate ways the Kingdom of God' (Article VI)?

This is not, of course, a distinctively Scottish problem. The controversy surrounding the Falklands Service in St Paul's Cathedral showed how acute are the tensions generated when some people see the church's role as celebration of national events and summing up of national feeling, while the churches must profess a higher loyalty which necessarily relativizes national pretensions. But there is an absolute need, if we are to speak to the nation, for the church not to be seen as detached, uninvolved, or even disloyal.

(*d*) Finally, should the church speak *for* the poor, the weak, and the marginalized, for those who have no voice of their own? Bias to the poor is a slogan much bandied about today, which is challenging, biblical, authentic. But it is not easy for declining churches which as they decline fall increasingly into a kind of bourgeois captivity to see this slogan as more than rhetoric. The church is strongest in the prosperous suburbs, in the universities (or some of them), in the fee-paying schools, and weakest in areas of deprivation and among the poor. The alienation of the poor from the churches is for us a major obstacle in the way of exercising a preferential option for the poor; it is hard for the church to speak for the poor because the church has so little firsthand knowledge of what the poor want to say. Before one can speak for someone else one has to listen, and how do the British churches listen to the poor, especially when the tone of what they hear is angry and suggests that the churches themselves are part of the problem, and that we must set our own house in order?

It is without doubt difficult. But not impossible. Because the church is still *there* in the urban priority areas and among the poor, although often a fragile and tenuous presence, there is listening and hearing going on. David Sheppard and David Jenkins are only two prominent examples chosen from many whose pastoral experience, whose listening, whose attempts to read the signs of the times, have led them into speaking for the poor. It is surprising sociologically that so much of this speaking for the voiceless goes on in our depleted and middle-class churches. But it is also profoundly encouraging.

The powerful can speak for themselves. They do not need the church to do the job for them, although they warmly welcome churchly and theological support and are vigorous in recruiting it. The powerful usually lay down what is accepted as 'possible', and present the defence of their interests as 'realism'. A part, and a central part, of the theological task is to redefine possibilities, to open things out, to increase the number of options, to restore hope to those who are condemned by 'realism' to a perpetuation of oppression. As Charles Elliott has effectively argued, we do not know what is possible until we have tried it (Elliott 1978: 178).

Liberation theologians firmly and very properly remind us that it is not enough to speak *for* the poor, and that to do so is fraught with dangers—of arrogance, of empty rhetoric, of the kind of cheap statement of general principles which the *Kairos Document* denounces as 'Church theology'. It is necessary to allow and enable the poor to speak for themselves, to say their piece. We cannot assume the right to speak for them. They must be empowered to speak for themselves, perhaps ultimately in the church, and through the church.

To Whom does the Church Speak?

When churches or theologians speak they rarely seem to ask whether anyone is listening. Is anyone listening? The answer not infrequently must be 'No'. Only too often church statements are a way of discharging conscience rather than getting anything done, or anything stopped. It would be good if those who issue statements on behalf of the churches asked about targeting: to whom is the statement addressed?

Some statements are primarily addressed to the members of the church and are intended to educate them and alert them to the issues for Christians involved in a particular situation, or to challenge them to scrutinize the way in which their assumptions and interests affect their way of looking at things. This is the church or theology exercising their pastoral and teaching offices. It is no accident that the US Catholic bishops issue *pastoral* letters on war and peace and on the economy. Pastoring the flock necessarily involves helping them to exercise their responsibilities, varied as they are, in a Christian way. And unless there is a great deal of this sort of educational effort going on within the church so that it becomes a kind of forum for moral and Christian examination of public affairs, it is hard to see in what sense church leaders may be seen as articulating the *consensus fidelium* in any sense.

As a legitimate extension of this pastoral and educational function, a church statement may be addressed to the public at large, challenging people to look at issues *sub specie aeternitatis*, drawing attention to factors often forgotten, reminding voters of the long-term implications of particular policies, and suggesting that immediate group or national interests do not give adequate guidance in the public sphere any more than in the private realm. The churches are still capable of reaching a huge number of people, and being listened to. One wonders whether they always use this access to the greatest effect, remembering that it is indeed an opportunity to witness to the truth of the gospel.

Other statements are directed primarily to decision-makers, seeking to give them guidance, understanding, and sometimes challenge in the exercise of their responsibilities. In the next chapter we examine some of the problems and possibilities in this particular area. Suffice it to say at this point that if we attend to the example of Jesus, his solace and encouragement was for the most part given to the weak and poor and marginalized. The powerful and the decision-makers tended to find him a disturbing and disconcerting presence. Theology's public statements should probably reflect the same qualities. We return to these questions in more detail in the next chapter.

A particular statement may, of course, be addressed to various audiences. Another of the virtues of the US Catholic bishops' 'Pastoral Letter on War and Peace' is that it makes remarkably clear at each stage who is addressed in particular, and in its final sections makes quite specific comments to various identified groups, suggesting what considerations each should take into account in undertaking its peculiar responsibilities. But only too frequently the diffuse generality which characterizes some church statements is rooted in an uncertainty about who is being addressed.

Church statements are surely intended to effect something —to change attitudes, to influence the way people vote, to affect decisions. But do they in fact make any difference? Only when church statements are clearly and cogently argued, make a distinctive contribution to the discussion, are accurately targeted, and followed through are they likely to have much influence, to be heard, and to affect the way things go. And here, above all, there is a danger of what Bonhoeffer called 'speaking the Word of God to excess' (Bonhoeffer 1954: 94), compulsively commenting on every item in the public agenda, and assuming that because it is the church that is speaking this is a *Christian* contribution to debate (rather than simply indifferent journalistic commentary on current affairs) and expecting people to listen to this avalanche of material.

Ultimately it is the life of the church which plays a major role in validating or denying the statements made. Only a church which is taking seriously the need for its own inner life to express the Kingdom and its righteousness can speak to the public domain with a right to be taken seriously. At the Sixth Assembly of the World Council of Churches in Vancouver in 1983 a Methodist minister from Sri Lanka spoke in a small group of the turmoil and the agony of his homeland. He described the history of mounting bitterness between the

Sinhalese Buddhist majority—some 80 per cent of the population—and the Tamil, largely Hindu, minority. He spoke of
riots and killings, of denials of fundamental rights, of murders
in gaols, of hatred and suspicion between the communities.
And then he spoke of the role of the churches in Sri Lanka:
together a tiny and almost powerless minority, but none the
less holding in fellowship, in trust, in love, Tamils and
Sinhalese in the same body. We heard how our friend, one of
the quiet and modest saints of this age, together with other
church leaders had again and again urged the government to
work for reconciliation between the two communities; repeatedly they had pointed out that without just treatment and
basic rights for all no lasting harmony is possible; in public and
in private they had warned that outbursts of violence were
inevitable unless there was a new and costly commitment to
peace and justice. No Buddhist Sinhalese monk would join
their deputations; no Hindu priest or swami dared approach
the Buddhist-dominated government. And many Christians,
clergy and lay, were in gaol for peacemaking. The next day our
Sinhalese friend was not in the group. He had been called away
by a cable which had arrived from Colombo: 'Your presence
urgently required as a peacemaker in Sri Lanka'. He left behind
a paper which he was unable to deliver. In it he said this:

In the eyes of the nation, the Christians divided into Roman Catholic,
Anglican, Methodist, Church of South India, Baptist, Presbyterian
and a host of other sects, unable to work in co-operation or to speak
the word of unity to themselves, can have no right to speak about
national reconciliation. The Church's lack of will to overcome its
own divisions is a scandalous impediment of its witness to the nation
. . . a divided Church loses its right to minister to the nation. Thus to
the Church in Sri Lanka the unity of the Church and the renewal,
unity and reconciliation of humankind is an indivisible whole.

In any setting the ability of the church to minister to the
nation depends on the seriousness with which it seeks to
exemplify in its own life the message it proclaims.

5

CONFRONTATION OR COLLUSION WITH THE POWERS?

When Jim Wallis and colleagues and friends from the Sojourners Community hold an unauthorized prayer meeting beneath the central dome of the Capitol in Washington DC to protest against the military budget, they believe they are confronting in the most effective and appropriate manner possible, evil and idolatry in its very temple (Wallis 1983: 127 ff.). When a group of radical British Christians, led by priests and religious, meet at the gate of a nuclear base to conduct a rite of exorcism they believe themselves to be confronting the powers which hold sway in that place. They understand themselves to be engaging in a profound way with the powers, with political evil. They see what they are doing as an act which unmasks and challenges the spiritual evil which haunts nuclear weaponry, the spiritual wickedness of which the bombs and missiles are the outward symbols and instruments.

To most people in this secular age, because we no longer believe in demons and spiritual forces, an exorcism seems quaint, anachronistic, and quite irrelevant to the hard realities for which the base stands. For the majority of onlookers the exorcism arouses amusement, or perhaps some temporary embarrassment. But these little groups of protesting Christians represent one more or less continuous strain of Christian political witness. In describing the evangelism of the early church Harnack wrote: 'It was as exorcisers that Christians went out into the great world, and exorcism formed one very powerful method of their mission and propaganda. It was a question not simply of exorcising and vanquishing the demons that dwelt in individuals, but also of purifying all public life from them' (Harnack 1904–5: i. 160–1). Spiritual wickedness in high places, some Christians continue to believe, is to be named as such, exposed, and thereby exorcized and deprived of its power. But does such 'confrontation with the powers' continue as a perennial option for Christians? Is it relevant in the modern world? Does it in fact achieve anything, or point to some truth?

At the other extreme, as an example of collusion with the powers, we may instance Winnington-Ingram, Bishop of London during the First World War. He proclaimed from the heart of the British power élite that the nation was engaged in a crusade, and declared that it was the Christian duty of every able-bodied man to fight for his God and country. In a letter to the *Guardian* in 1915 he wrote that it was the Church's task 'TO MOBILISE THE NATION FOR A HOLY WAR', and in a now notorious Advent sermon delivered the same year he called on soldiers 'to kill the good as well as the bad, to kill the young men as well as the old' (Hastings 1986: 45). Memories like that cause at least as much embarrassment among Christians today as an exorcism at a nuclear base. Is it perhaps a true instinct which makes Christians uneasy with such extremes and suspicious of too great readiness without qualification to identify any political purpose with good or evil? Yet the middle ground, with its pitfalls and hazards, must be understood in relation to the extremes. Accordingly in this chapter we explore the ways in which Christians may properly relate to the powers in a Christian way.

The Powers are People and should be Treated as Such

That is an important dimension of the truth. And it has implications which we need to examine. The powers, the suggestion is, are demystified and rendered intelligible and manageable when we discover that they are just people like ourselves. 'Leviathan', declared John Macmurray in a memorable passage, 'is not merely a monster but a fabulous monster; the creature of a terrified imagination. If we track the State to his lair, what shall we find? Merely a collection of overworked and worried gentlemen, not at all unlike ourselves, doing their best to keep the machinery of government working as well as may be, and hard put to it to keep up appearances' (Macmurray 1961: 200). How then should one approach this demystified monster, these overworked and worried gentlemen not at all unlike ourselves?

An answer which presupposes Macmurray's interpretation of the situation was provided by that redoubtable ecumenical statesman, J. H. Oldham, who is (incorrectly) believed to have said, 'Find out who the Powers are and take them to lunch in the Athenaeum.' But that saying captures the essence of Oldham's highly effective strategy for bringing Christian influence to bear in the places that really matter. The assumption is that one can do business with 'people like us', with one's own kind. There is a groundwork of shared assumptions, common experience, and commitment to similar goals which makes the lunch in the Athenaeum not only enjoyable in itself, but frequently productive in affecting the way things go. It is reassuring to discover that Leviathan is a pantomime monster; inside its skin are people like us, who deserve our sympathy, with whom it is not difficult to do business because we have so much in common. To attempt to exorcize them would hardly be good form!

It is, however, necessary to recognize that these overworked and worried gentlemen, like us, have needs, responsibilities, and limitations. Like us, they need encouragement, support, and pastoral care. It is in itself perfectly proper and desirable that there should be chaplains to the powerful, pastors who have the necessary empathy, insight, and experience to minister to those who carry great responsibilities. A pastor's task, however, is never to collude in the games people play, or allow people to remain in a comforting but unreal world of fantasy. A proper pastoral care involves constant, sometimes painful, probing below the surface to find and unmask what hidden motivations lurk beneath—interests, pathologies, and fears which can distort judgement and action at their spring. Such is true pastoral support, the authentic ministry to the powerful.

These people also have their distinctive responsibilities. In politics the patterns of responsibility are peculiarly complex. Politics as the art of the possible involves compromise. Politicians cannot work miracles, or render the human condition unproblematic. They know that often pathetically excessive hopes are invested in their activities. But that does not mean that the true responsibility of these worried and overworked gentlemen whose intentions are so good is simply to keep the machine running, making adjustments, and wielding the oil-can as and when required. The usual theory is that the machine runs according to its own principles; most kinds of interference are dangerous and counter-productive. It needs servicing from time to time, but not replacement. Hence the powerful generally see their responsibilities in terms of accepting and running the system. For most of the worried and overworked gentlemen acceptance of the system involves neither having too grandiose expectations of what it might deliver, nor fearing it as a demonic force. But surely their real responsibilities go beyond the difficult decisions and moral ambiguities involved in keeping the system running. There needs to be an ongoing critique of the system and its adequacy in the light of a larger vision of what politics is about, and the significance of the issues at stake.

Furthermore, these overworked and worried gentlemen, like the rest of us, have their limitations. They have their own distinctive knowledge, it is true; knowledge of the complexity of the decisions they have to take, knowledge that most of their choices are between second-bests, knowledge of their own incapacity to achieve the ideal. But too frequently they also are ignorant of how people affected by their decisions live, are too enclosed in clubland or the senior common room. And, like the rest of us, they are sinners, subject to the corrupting influence of power. Good intentions and idealism, combined with hard work, are not enough. The powerful need to be helped by the church to resist the specific temptations that go with their responsibilities.

The church needs to minister to these people in the fulfilment of their responsibilities and in their limitations and sin. The powerful need pastors who appreciate the complexity of the problems facing them, but nevertheless challenge and enlarge their sense of responsibility. They need, according to John Habgood, two kinds of help—help in holding to a simple vision, and help in actually handling the contradictions and conflicts on the road (Habgood 1983: 106). Like all of us, they need forgiveness and encouragement.

Ministry to the powerful involves special dangers: the danger of being sucked into collusion in particular, so that the pastor can never question or confront. But such dangers are no excuse for avoiding the responsibility of a ministry to the powerful which is at the same time pastoral and prophetic.

The Powers are Impersonal Structures and Spiritual Forces, and should be Treated as Such

To personalize the powers, to say that the state is nothing more than 'a collection of overworked and worried gentlemen, not at all unlike ourselves', is a dangerous half-truth. The stock market is not the sum of the stockbrokers and investors taking part in it, nor is the state simply a group of busy people. Any major social institution transcends the individuals who compose it, and transforms their conscious purposes. It is easy to understand why we like to say that the state is just this group of individuals; it is easier to understand and relate to, especially if we assume that all the system requires for its adequate working is the odd adjustment here, or bit of fine tuning there.

But 'people like us' can run demonic systems. That is the lesson that we should have learned from Nazi Germany, from apartheid South Africa, from many of the countries of Latin America, from some of the involvements of academics in the Vietnam War. Decent folk can be caught up and swept along by the evils of a system, often without realizing what is happening until it is too late. It is salutory to remember, for example, that the officers of the *Einsatzgruppen* which carried out the mass murder of Jews, communists, and other 'undesirables' on the Eastern Front under Heydrich were 'a representative cross-section of well-educated, respectable Germans in the Third Reich'. The commander of *Einsatzgruppe D* had been the research director of an economics institute in Kiel. Another had been a Lutheran pastor (Rubenstein and Roth 1987: 128–9). And intellectuals in many contexts have shown themselves remarkably adept at disguising with words the true nature of evil courses to which they are committed.

When Adolf Harnack, the very epitome of the nineteenth-century liberal theologian, wrote the passage quoted earlier, about exorcizing the demons in public life, he was describing as a faithful historian the way the early Christians saw their relationship to the public realm. Personally he clearly had no time for the world-view that underlay this way of looking at the public realm. Liberal theologians often had sympathies with Hegelian notions of history as the drama of the evolution of *Geist*, and saw the state as a moral entity transcending its citizens, a manifestation of Spirit. But such ideas were believed to belong to a quite different plane from the primitive belief that the world was full of demons and angels, of principalities and powers, of thrones and dominions. Such language occurs plentifully in the New Testament. But for Harnack and his like it was part of the disposable time-bound husk which must be cast away if the eternal gospel of the fatherhood of God and the brotherhood of man (*sic*) was to shine through clearly in all its purity and attractiveness.

Early attempts to study the place of spiritual powers in the thought of St Paul had aroused little general interest (Everling 1888: Dibelius 1909). It was only when face to face with Hitler, attempting to interpret theologically what was happening and respond to events in the light of the New Testament that some people, particularly Karl Barth and his circle, turned with a new expectation and excitement to the language of 'the powers' in the New Testament. There they found passages about the 'rulers of this age', who do not understand the purposes of God, who have 'crucified the King of glory', but are 'doomed to pass away' (1 Cor. 2: 6–8). In Christ, they read, God has 'disarmed' the principalities and powers and made a public example of them, triumphing over them (Col. 2: 15). And, with a change of tense, Christ *will* dethrone every power (1 Cor. 15: 24–6), and put them into subjection, for they were created by him and for him (Col. 1: 16). In this subjection to Christ the powers are restored to their proper role, function, and limits. Their demonic pretensions are curbed and they become what they properly are, what they were created to be, 'ministering spirits sent forth to serve' (Heb. 1: 14).

These texts suggest that those who have not yet died with Christ to the elemental spirits of the universe and still live in a worldly way tend to worship angels and powers rather than God himself. They accept and collude in the extravagant pretensions of the powers and cannot see beyond them. But believers and the church are called upon to do three things in relation to the powers. First, they must struggle against the principalities and powers, 'against the world rulers of this present darkness, against the spiritual hosts of wickedness in the heavenly places' (Eph. 6: 12). Secondly, and only superficially in tension with the first, Christians are to be subject to the powers, to honour and respect them, because they have been established by God and derive their authority, whether they recognize this or not, from him. The powers cannot escape from the fact that they are God's servants—nor can we. Thirdly, the church is the channel through which the manifold wisdom of God is to be made known to the principalities and powers (Eph. 3: 10). The church, in other words, has a message for, and a responsibility towards, the powers because they have a significant role in God's design. And in all their dealings with the powers Christians are sustained by the knowledge that God's purposes cannot ultimately be frustrated.

For Barth and his colleagues this material in the epistles, and similar passages in the gospels and Revelation, gave vital clues for a proper understanding of the political realm and the church's responsibilities towards it. The state belongs to Jesus Christ and should serve him. It is to be understood christologically. By renouncing its true origin and destiny the state may become demonic, but even so it cannot escape from the pressure of its divine commission, and its demonic purposes are doomed to frustration. Because the state figures so prominently in God's purposes, 'the most brutally unjust State cannot lessen the Church's responsibility for the State; indeed it can only increase it' (Barth 1939: 64). The political order is charged with profound spiritual significance. In confronting head-on the evils of Nazism, those who were nourished by this way of thinking could still see in the Third Reich a divine order which had been radically perverted, and which needed to be restored. Confronting such a regime and recalling it to its true role is a special responsibility for Christians because they alone have a knowledge of the christological foundation and the divine mandate of the state. They have been emancipated from thraldom to principalities and powers, set free to deal with the state and its responsibilities realistically, constantly aware of the deep spiritual significance of these things. They are not relating to a system which is spiritually neutral. The state has a place of great importance in God's purposes. We must then affirm the dignity of the powers, their role in God's plan, their tendency to rebellion, and the ultimate futility of that rebellion. The powers have a proper claim on respect, co-operation, obedience, prayers, and criticism. Clear boundaries are set. It is not just Hitler or Stalin who is to be understood in this way.

It is also 'the collection of overworked and worried gentlemen, not at all unlike ourselves' who, despite appearances, are principalities and powers—or at least ministering spirits!

The exegetical base for this way of regarding the state was developed, particularly by Oscar Cullmann (Cullmann 1951, 1957). During the ascendancy of the 'biblical theology' movement in the 1950s it became almost a received orthodoxy. The language of principalities and powers was widely regarded as the proper symbolic structure to enable Christians to understand the political realm, and relate to it in a Christian way (t'Hooft 1948; Stewart 1951; Macgregor 1954; Berkhof, 1953, ET 1962; Caird, 1956). More recently, in a Cambridge monograph written in the very different circumstances of England in the 1980s, Wesley Carr has argued that the 'curious notion that behind the rulers stand angelic beings is misguided'. Paul's ethical thought, he believes, does not need 'recourse to an obscure mythology' because it is realistic, accepts 'the facts of social life', and is apparently only loosely related to his theology (Carr 1981: 175).

Carr's book provoked a powerful rejoinder from an American scholar, Walter Wink, to whom it was sent for review. Wink had been exposed to, and deeply challenged by, the Latin American context from which Liberation Theology springs. Wink finds the New Testament to be full of the language of power and on the whole he endorses and develops the line of interpretation we have traced back to Barth and Cullmann. He does not see Paul's ethic and world-view as conservative, but believes the language of principalities and powers to be perennially illuminating. This view had been forced upon him by his encounter with poverty, oppression, and injustice in Latin America. Wink suggests that the New Testament has a remarkable awareness of the pervasiveness, concreteness, and spiritual and moral ambiguity of power. He argues that 'the "principalities and powers" are the inner and outer aspects of any given manifestation of power' (Wink 1984: 5). This means that:

The New Testament's 'principalities and powers' is a generic category referring to the determining forces of physical, psychic, and social existence. These powers usually consist of an outer manifestation and an inner spirituality or interiority. Power must become incarnate, institutionalized or systemic in order to be effective. It has a dual aspect, possessing both an outer, visible form (constitutions, judges, police, leaders, office complexes), and an inner, invisible spirit that provides it legitimacy, compliance, credibility, and clout. (Wink 1986: 4)

When powers become idolatrous, Wink continues, through denying their mandate and placing themselves above God's good purposes for humankind they become demonic, and the church's task is to unmask this idolatry and recall the powers to their task. Institutions, he suggests, have their inwardness, their spirituality, which determines how their power is used. Hence in their dealings with the political and economic orders Christians are not simply concerned with structural change and with material things, but with the spiritual dimension.

Our group of overworked and worried gentlemen, if one accepts this line of argument, are not only parts of a system, but a system which expresses a spirituality which can become idolatrous. It has to be judged not solely, or even mainly, in terms of the personal moral integrity of the 'gentlemen' who run it, but in terms of the functions, effects, and pretensions of the system.

How as Christians do we relate to the Powers, how does the Church relate to the Powers, constantly aware that what the Powers do concerns the Kingdom that the Church proclaims, and that the Church, in Barth's words, 'is responsible for the State and for Caesar'? (Barth 1939: 11)

We must never forget that in our society the church and the powers are not entirely separate and distinct. Many of the overworked and worried gentlemen running things are Christians, trying very seriously, as often as not, to relate their faith to their secular responsibilities. Denunciations, or exhortations for that matter, from those who have not troubled to appreciate the complexity of the issues they face are unhelpful, to say the least.

To be among the powerful and influential is not in itself to collude with the principalities and powers. But the danger of being sucked into collusion is great whenever one ceases to monitor what one is doing in a Christian way, to hold one's responsibilities in the system as responsibilities before God, and to live from God's grace and forgiveness. There are, of course, situations where Christians should withdraw from the system and witness against it by so doing. Paul Oestreicher gives the instance of his grandfather, who was a deputy prison governor in Germany, politically an arch-conservative and a man of deep principle. Soon after the Nazis came to power he noticed that a new kind of prisoner was now being consigned to his custody, people he could not but regard as innocent, communists, Jews, and gypsies. After a short period of unavailing complaints and protest, he resigned as a matter of principle. The prison system had been perverted (Oestreicher 1986: 31). The only way of maintaining integrity, he believed, was to withdraw. To have stayed in office would have become collusion with the powers of darkness. Archbishop Romero identified a similar crisis when before his martyrdom he pointed to the impossibility of working within the power structures of El Salvador: 'It is in practice illegal', he wrote, 'to be an authentic Christian in our environment . . . precisely because the world around us is founded radically on an established disorder before which the mere proclamation of the gospel is subversive' (quoted in Elliott 1987: 134).

These, one might say, are extreme examples, remote from the kind of situations which we face. And there is truth in that comment. But for us too there must be a point where the necessary compromises of politics and the inevitability of dirty hands shades into collusion with evil. And Christians must be vigilant to discern when this is happening, alert to their responsibilities, and aware where their ultimate allegiance lies.

The powers, we read in the Bible, have been unmasked as false gods by their encounter with the true God. They are made a public spectacle, defeated, and then restored to their proper function and dignity. Unmasking, however, is not the simple realization that the powers, after all, are nothing but a collection of overworked and worried gentlemen like us. If, for example, you unmask the international monetary system you discover, first of all, that it is charging Africa some 30 per cent of the value of its exports simply to service its debts—and this at a time when the pressing need of these countries is for vast inflows of capital. Who is responsible? That question is peculiarly difficult to answer. Responsibility is diffused through the banks and finance ministries of all the wealthy countries. No small group of individuals controls the system and can be held responsible for its working. But most of those involved in the rich countries do not even believe that the system *is* vicious and needs to be changed. Because it serves their interests they feel comfortable with it. They need to have their eyes opened to the realities. They need to confront the unmasked powers, and realize that the international monetary system is not divine and immutable (Elliott 1987: 154; George 1988). Responsibility may be diffused within the world economic system. But there *is* responsibility there, and it is primarily laid on the shoulders of the rich and powerful—individuals, organizations, and nations.

Finally, a word on confronting the powers without necessarily denouncing or damning the people who work the system, or suggesting that they have more freedom, responsibility, or ability to change things than is in fact the case. We have much to learn from Mahatma Gandhi here. He had a rare ability to maintain friendship and relations of mutual respect with his antagonists, with the collection of overworked and worried gentlemen who ran the Raj, while confronting in an unqualified way the system that they ran. He developed a 'saintly idiom' in politics and constantly affirmed that in political struggles profound spiritual issues were at stake. The 'naked fakir' striding up the steps of the Viceregal Palace was not simply an embarrassing official visitor exercising a sophisticated kind of moral blackmail; he was respected, admired, trusted, a friend, if a disturbing one.

Gandhi's colleague, the remarkable Christian missionary C. F. Andrews, was given by Gandhi the task of ending the evil system of indentured labour, which amounted very often to virtual slavery, a system that could well be labelled a 'principality and power'. Andrews's distinctive style of confronting the powers is indicated by his meeting with Sir Gordon Guggisberg, about to become Governor of British Guiana, where there were large numbers of Indian indentured labourers. Alek Fraser, the great missionary statesman, arranged a meeting for the two men in the Army and Navy Club. He described the encounter thus:

I was with Sir Gordon when the porter came and said that there was a man at the door who said he had an appointment with him, but he had not liked to let him in until Sir G. saw him. I said 'That's Charlie'. It was. It was summer time, and he had on sand-shoes (plimsoles), flannel bags, a very ancient woollen knitted waistcoat, a frayed cricket shirt, a wisp of a tie, and an ancient black coat—the worst I had seen on him. We sat down at a central table, and Admirals, Generals, Governors, etc. came and spoke to Sir Gordon, glad to see him back in the Club. He introduced us to all. Then we had a long chat in an alcove. Then G. took Charlie down to the street as C. had to go, put him in a taxi, paid for it, and sent him off. As the taxi rolled away, Sir Gordon gazed after it with bowed head and fixed eyes. It disappeared round a corner. G. breathed deeply and turned to me and said slowly 'I feel as though I had been honoured to give lunch to Our Lord'. (cited in Tinker 1979: 231)

That might provide a kind of model of how Christians may relate most effectively to the powers, speaking truth to power in love.

6

MYSTIQUE AND POLITIQUE

or

How to Sing the Lord's Song in a Strange Land

In this final chapter, as in the first, we start with a parable:

The Skylark and the Frogs

Once upon a time a community of frogs lived at the bottom of a deep, damp well, into which no light penetrated from the outside world. Their king, the great Boss Frog, claimed to own the well and all within it. He ordered the other frogs around, but never did any work himself and expected the bottom-dog frogs to provide for all his needs and wishes. The poor bottom-dog frogs spent all their days, and much of their nights as well, searching in the mud and slime for the worms and grubs which the Boss Frog devoured, making him fat and sleek.

From time to time a stray skylark would find its way down into the well, and hovering just above the frogs' heads it would sing to them sweetly of the wonders of the world outside: the warming glory of the sun, the cool beauty of the moon; the great mountains, covered with heather, rearing skywards; the mighty seas, decked with spume and full of strange creatures; the fertile farmlands and the vast cities in which human beings lived crowded together in communities; and how all these wonders were laid below the little bird that soared in the limitless skies.

The Boss Frog told the bottom-dog frogs that they should listen carefully to the song of the skylark. 'Because', the Boss Frog would explain, 'it is teaching you about a happy land far away to which all good frogs go when they die and depart from this damp, dark well.' But in his heart the Boss Frog, who did not understand the lark's song at all, believed that the bird was quite insane.

Although they were respectful in public, the bottom-dog frogs did not really believe what the Boss Frog said. But they had also with time grown suspicious of the sweet song of the skylark, and believed that the bird was off its head and had lost all touch with reality. Besides, some free-thinking frogs among them argued that the skylark was little more than an agent of the Boss Frog, encouraging them to be docile and hard-working with tales of pie in the sky that you get when you die. 'And that's a lie', they muttered resentfully.

Then there arose a philosopher among the bottom-dog frogs, who presented a new and intriguing interpretation of the skylark's song. 'The song is not simply false, nor is it insane', he said. 'In its strange, distorted way the lark is telling us what a splendid place we might make this well if we took our destiny into our own hands. When the skylark sings of the sun and the moon, it is really telling us we could install electric lighting in our dark well, and fill it with brightness. When it sings of the winds and the waves and the cool fir forests, it is really telling us that by ventilation we could transform the atmosphere, and replace the foul mists of our well with bracing, pine-scented breezes. The lark's tale of soaring in the limitless skies is a poetic way of speaking of the delights which could be ours if we were not forced to devote our lives to such dull, uncreative, and alienating labour to keep the Boss Frog fed and happy. Above all, this talk of flying points to the freedom we shall all enjoy when the oppression of the Boss Frog is removed for ever. The bird is not to be despised. Its song inspires us to seek a revolutionary improvement of our lot.'

The bottom-dog frogs were convinced by the philosopher-frog's interpretation of the skylark's visits and the meaning of its song. They attended to the skylark very intently whenever it fluttered down into the well. And when the revolution came, the bottom-dog frogs marched to the barricades croaking as best they could an imitation of the skylark's song, and bearing banners with the skylark's image on them. The Boss Frog and his cronies were overthrown, and after a series of major reforms the well was transformed by the introduction of lighting and ventilation and all sorts of modern comforts and delights, making it a congenial place fit for frogs to live in—just as the philosopher-frog had prophesied.

But *still* the disturbing skylark would swoop down into the thoroughly modernized well, singing of the sun and the moon and the stars, of mountains and valleys and seas, and of the great vistas of the outside world.

'Perhaps', suggested the philosopher-frog, 'this bird *is* mad, after all. Surely we have no further need of these cryptic songs. And in any case, it is very tiresome to have to listen to fantasies when the fantasies have lost their social relevance.'

So one day the frogs managed to catch the lark in a trap. Then they killed it, stuffed it, and put it in their newly built civic museum . . . in a place of honour.

Yet, even so, the skylark continued more frequently than ever to swoop down into the well and make the frogs restless and delighted with its sweet song of the boundless world above . . .

(This is a paraphrase and adapted version of the parable as told by Roszak 1970: 121–3)

The lark's song—'the Lord's song in a strange land' (Ps. 137: 4)—speaks of a message which perennially disturbs and challenges all systems and orders, even the best, by setting alongside them the reality of the Kingdom. It puts the well, the 'strange' land, and all that goes on there under question precisely by setting it in its proper perspective. It is not a self-contained system. Hearing the lark's song makes the well a strange land to those who dwell in it. There is that beyond the well which alone gives what happens there its true significance. The message involves a vast enlargement of horizons, challenging the realism of the well with a broader view of reality. The well, with its mud and slime, and awful Boss Frog, is not all that there is, or all one may hope for.

The message comes in the indicative mood. It tells of mountains, skies, and seas, poetic perhaps, but descriptive of realities beyond the frogs' ken. It is an account of reality which calls for a response. It is not on the surface an ethical or political message, but it has political implications, although there is far more to it than that. It is a song particularly prone to abuse and misinterpretation, as the parable makes clear. It may be interpreted as providing a rationale for conformity, resignation, and unquestioning obedience: the 'happy land' is then seen as entirely and exclusively the place of posthumous reward. Or the song may be transposed into the notation of a political ideology to be implemented by specific policies. But the skylark's song must not be 'impaled and bent into an ideological instrument' (Edwin Muir 1960: 228), for to do so destroys it in its authentic wholeness.

And yet the lark's song is about 'home', about the authentic nature and destiny of 'frogs'. It does have political content and political implications. The problem is how to attend to, interpret, and respond to this song in our 'strange land', without distorting or manipulating its message.

The Language of Transcendence

The song is in a different language from that of frogs, or politicians, or policy-makers, for that matter. But the two languages are not unconnected; indeed they *need* one another.

But why is the language of transcendence, *this* language of transcendence, necessary? Without it, in the first place, politics is distorted. Too many hopes come to be invested in politics, as if the right policies, implemented effectively, would be capable of rendering the human condition unproblematic. People look to politics for what it cannot on its own deliver: a sense of meaning, of belonging, of significance. In effect the limits are removed from politics, and the political process is invested with the divine attributes of omnipotence and omniscience. As Michael Ignatieff points out, 'There is much that we can suffer which justice, equality and fraternity can redeem, but there is much else that we cannot do anything about: illness, ageing, separation and death. True enough, some societies help individuals to bear these burdens with greater dignity than others . . . Yet the sharing of suffering can only distribute the burden' (Ignatieff 1984: 100). Politics on its own cannot provide the kind of ultimate meaning which people long for, and which is a fundamental human need. As Solzhenitsyn tried to show in his novel, *Cancer Ward*, even the most compelling of this-worldly ideologies is silent in face of death. Without a vital language of transcendence providing some hints and clues to the mystery of life and enabling people to explore that mystery with confidence, titanic politics flourishes, politics embarks on the futile project of itself providing what only faith can offer—a horizon of meaning, significance, and hope. Such politics plunders the language of transcendence to invest the market or the polity with an alien numinosity, borrowing the great symbols of transcendence to make us worship that which is not God, and expect 'heaven on earth' as the result of the benign workings of the market or the state. With the decline in the modern world of the language of transcendence, too heavy a demand is put upon earthly politics to provide meaning and justification, and in endeavouring to do so politics is perverted (Ramsey 1968: 14–18).

Alternatively, politics becomes mere horse-trading, 'Who gets what, when and how' (Lasswell 1958), deprived of any kind of broader significance, and indeed believed to be independent of ethics. As Max Horkheimer wrote: 'A politics which, even when highly unreflected, does not preserve a theological moment in itself is, no matter how skilful, in the last analysis, mere business' (in Davis 1980: 133). But the history of recent times does not suggest that politics as 'mere business' can be sustained for long; it quickly tips over into politics-as-idolatry.

The language of transcendence relating to politics is necessary, in the second place, if faith itself is not to be distorted. There is substance to E. R. Norman's charge that the churches have sometimes taken over secular radical ideologies (or conservative ideologies for that matter—a point Norman seriously neglects) and presented them as the gospel (Norman 1979). When this happens, people quickly discover that it is a partial and distorted gospel that is being offered, and that it is simpler, and more honest, to go directly to the secular ideology for guidance, disregarding the pious embellishments.

E. R. Norman attacks an unconscious accommodation to the spirit of the age; Oliver O'Donovan has pointed to a tendency in the Church of England and elsewhere consciously and deliberately to set aside the language of transcendence when contributing to public debate. His close examination of the report on divorce-law reform, *Putting Asunder* (1966), revealed a principle which is clearly now widely operative elsewhere as well: 'When the church contributes to public debate on matters of concern to society at large, it should forget that it is the church of Jesus Christ and should address society in terms common to all participants. The attempt to be distinctively Christian belongs only to the pursuit of internal discipline among the faithful' (O'Donovan 1986: 20). In order to ensure that they are heard, Christians must accommodate themselves to secular perspectives, set aside any distinctive language of transcendence, and cease to base arguments on theological premises. 'Any advice that the church renders to the state', *Putting Asunder* averred, 'must rest not upon doctrines that only Christians accept, but upon premises that enjoy wide acknowledgement in the nation as a whole' (BSR 1966: 17). But too much, surely, can be sacrificed to gain a hearing. And if theology simply reiterates what everyone is saying already, no one will listen.

There is apparently no such thing as a *general* language of transcendence, despite the attempts of various people to suggest that only such a language may be deployed in a plural society in place of languages and concepts which belong to one particular religious system. Christian theology is one specific language of transcendence which, like other specific languages of transcendence, resists being distilled into a general idiom of transcendence, acceptable to all.

If what theology has to say in no significant way differs from what most people are saying anyway, theology and the church lose credibility; they should either have kept silent, or said something distinctive, rooted in their own convictions about God, human beings, and fellowship. 'Only a church which speaks with the world's voice is likely to be heard by the world,' writes John Habgood, 'but how can it then escape worldliness?' (Habgood 1983: 54). How indeed!

Let us consider the case of the Report on the Archbishop's Commission on Urban Priority Areas, *Faith in the City* (Archbishop's Commission, 1985). This report will certainly appear in the history books as a milestone in the church's contribution to public affairs. In a way the Commission did speak with the world's voice. It was organized more or less like a Royal Commission. Its chairman was a distinguished public servant. The Commission was serviced and its report written by a senior civil servant on secondment. Despite its initially hostile reception from the government, there is no doubt at all that it contributed vastly to the realization in all sections of the community of the urgency of the situation in the UPAs. It was heard, perhaps because it spoke with the world's voice. But there was no conscious rejection of theological reflection, as in *Putting Asunder* or in *Changing Britain*. There *were* theological sections in *Faith in the City*, although they gave the impression of being inserted somewhat artificially, rather than informing the whole analysis of the report. Frank Field declared, somewhat harshly

it could have been produced by any group of well-intentioned individuals. What should have made it special, and different from secular analyses, was its theology of God's vision of the world, the nature of man and his part in working out this design. However, instead of this being the starting point for the report, a theological perspective is merely tacked on to what is essentially a secular approach'. (Field 1985: 144)

A perceptive detailed critique of the theology of the Archbishop's Commission Report has now been provided by Nigel Biggar (Biggar 1988).

There *is* theology in *Faith in the City*; the best part of two chapters of it. But although some other sections of the report sound prophetic, and clearly share in the anger, frustration, and hopes of people in the UPAs, although most of the language is clear and direct, in the theological sections the language becomes tentative, detached, and almost apologetic — 'It may be argued . . .', 'It may be felt . . .', 'We may well be asked . . .', 'If the policies of any government can be shown to be making the plight of some classes of citizens actually worse . . . it is a clear duty for the Church to sound a warning that our society may be losing the "compassionate" character that is still desired by the majority of its members'. There are lots of nods in the direction of tolerance, consensus, community, and co-operation, but also a refusal to look conflicts of interest and social unrest in the face. These, we are told, are 'grey areas' with which theology finds great difficulty in engaging: 'We have little tradition of initiating conflict and coping with it creatively. We are not at home in the tough secular milieu of social and political activism' (p. 49). That honest and revealing remark points to the fundamental problem of modern British theology in this connection: its home is the senior common room or the seminary. It accordingly has peculiar difficulty in entering into productive dialogue with the influential social theories of today, whether associated with the New Right or with Marxism. Nor does it see its task as providing a useful resource for Christians seeking the signs of the Kingdom in today's world. There is little in these chapters of *Faith in the City* that might count as a distinctively Christian or theological insight into human nature, social relations, the understanding of history, or the interpretation of what is going on.

But, despite the inadequacies of this rather bland *explicit* theology, there is in *Faith in the City* another theology, an *implicit* theology which rarely appears on the surface but is undoubtedly influential in the shaping of the method and approach and conclusions of the report. This is, in fact, the working faith of intelligent, sensitive, and committed lay people such as those who served on the Commission. As a kind of 'Kingdom theology' this implicit theology provides an explanation of why the Commission found it so necessary to concern itself with 'secular' matters: the condition of the inner cities is an issue which has profound importance in relation to the city of God. Because people in the UPAs are the 'sheep without a shepherd' of today, the church must attend to the poor and the marginalized. And the report does not only concern itself with secular problems; it takes both the calling and the empirical reality of the church with profound seriousness. The Commission does not permit its sober and realistic assessment of the state of the church to obscure the fact that it is precisely *this* church which is called to be a sign and preliminary manifestation of the Kingdom of God. Only when the church is serious about setting its own house in order can it call on the state to do justly and love mercy.

There is no doubt that *Faith in the City* has been heard, and is still attended to, by 'the world'. But it is quite unfair to say that it speaks with the world's voice, or has capitulated to worldliness.

Translating the Song

But how may the language of transcendence, the Songs of Zion, be translated or deployed in debate about public policy in a secular age in this strange land? There seem to be three main possibilities: the Christian vision may be presented obliquely, indirectly—the only authentic way of presenting Christian truth, according to Søren Kierkegaard; or directly and confidently, as by Karl Barth or Reinhold Niebuhr, as providing the most adequate interpretation of reality, superior to all alternatives on offer; or, finally, in an apparently secular idiom, as it were, free from jargon and explicitly theological language, although the substance remains firmly rooted in Christian truth. Here our exemplar will be R. H. Tawney.

Kierkegaard's method was essentially socratic. The one who would communicate the truth must realize that the task is not to transfer or sell a package of something, but by questioning, discussion, and challenge to awaken the hearer, and thus enable an openness to the truth. That done, the teacher stands aside to allow a direct and responsible relationship between the hearer and the truth. In the context of our present concerns that suggests that theology's role is to ask the awkward and disturbing questions, to raise the issues most people would prefer to forget, to jolt people into looking at things in a different way, to encourage a reverence for truth and for people—and then to stand back, refusing to give answers, and affirming policy-makers' direct responsibility before God. The role is maieutic, not constructive. It is often confrontational, for the truth cannot be faced unless falsehood is unmasked. This kind of theology is consistently disturbing, for it believes that falsehoods and half-truths are easier to live with than the truth. Before this truth, which is incarnate in Jesus and those with whom he identifies, the powerful frequently fall back on Pilate's question, 'What is truth?' and turn to a simple pragmatic, or a cynical politics.

Karl Barth and Reinhold Niebuhr, for all their disagreements, shared an amazing confidence that Christianity provides the most adequate account of reality, that its truth makes it the best guide to responsible action. Correctly understood, they teach, Christianity must be preferred to all alternatives on offer. 'All the known facts of history', Niebuhr declared with characteristic boldness, 'verify the interpretation of human destiny implied in New Testament eschatology' (Niebuhr 1944, ii: 330). The robust Christian realism Niebuhr developed gave, he believed, a more adequate account of the heights and depths of human nature than optimistic liberalism or conservative pessimism. Despite—or because of—what many people see as arrogance, Niebuhr had a profound and lasting effect on American policy-makers, and on the academic discipline of international relations. Barth had a no less significant impact on discussions of Nazism, the Cold War, nuclear deterrence, and other matters far beyond the churches as well as inside. In their differing ways both Barth and Niebuhr saw their responsibility in the public realm as confessing the Christian faith, an evangelistic or apologetic task.

Tawney's approach was quite different. He lamented the extent to which theology and the Christian faith had evacuated the public realm. He believed that theology and the social sciences had parted company, to the impoverishment of both. His own task, along with William Temple and many others, was to bring theology back to engagement with the central issues of social life. He often spoke in terms of combating idolatry in economic and political life. But it is not always recognized how consciously and consistently Tawney sought to ground his thought in his Christian faith. Much of the evidence for this is to be found in his *Commonplace Book* (Tawney 1972), only published after his death. The works Tawney published during his lifetime contain less explicit theology as time goes on. Clearly this is not because Tawney was losing his Christian faith; he died a Christian, though a restless one, much discontented with the church. He struggled increasingly vigorously to communicate Christian truth in secular language as society became more secular and fewer people were comfortable with a religious idiom. Those who probe below the surface of a book such as *Equality* (1931) find motivation, insights, and values which are profoundly Christian. And he saw Christian values and insights as deeply opposed to the operative values and assumptions of modern capitalist society. His influence on social policy in Britain was, and is, immense.

Confessing the Faith in the Public Realm

The theologians we have discussed above all saw their task as in some sense confessing the faith in the public realm, acknowledging the lordship of Jesus Christ, and exercising power in the light of the truth that is to be found in him. This gives a sense of proportion to politics, and deeply influences one's set of priorities. In a way it is an apologetic and evangelistic project. It means that the Christian cannot set aside his or her fundamental convictions and take on board others when moving into the political arena. Christian convictions must be operative there, or they are valid nowhere. For it is here that the great idols of modern life flourish and call for our allegiance.

A series of important twentieth-century confessional statements with a direct bearing on political issues have shown an increasing unease with any suggestion that the political and economic spheres are autonomous and exempt from theological scrutiny, and a widespread recognition that statements of faith in fact have at least implicit political content. Confessional statements do not always require the mediation of ethics in order to become effective in politics; indeed there is a danger, as Eberhard Bethge the close friend and biographer of Dietrich Bonhoeffer notes, that saving faith may be dissolved into ethics (Duchrow 1987: p. x). In the political and economic spheres issues of idolatry arise, questions of where one's ultimate loyalty lies and issues, too, of responsibility and repentance. The great issues may often be technical and complex, but they are not *adiaphora*, matters indifferent, but often related to the very substance of the faith. Hence, so the argument goes, faithfulness to the Lord always involves commitment to justice and the values of the Kingdom and rejection of any attempt to put any system, ideology, or regime in the place of the Kingdom and its righteousness.

The classic instance of this sort of confessional statement was *The Theological Declaration of Barmen* (1934), formulated by Karl Barth and subscribed by those who were to become the leaders of the Confessing Church in Germany. The Declaration affirmed the truth of the gospel in such a way as to denounce Nazism as a new paganism, incompatible with Christian faith because it put the Führer, the nation, and the race in the place which should be accorded to Christ alone. They rejected the pretensions of the Nazi totalitarian state, and affirmed the liberty of the church:

We reject the false doctrine, as though the State, over and beyond its special commission, should and can become the single and totalitarian order of human life, thus fulfilling the Church's vocation as well. We reject the false notion, as though the Church, over and beyond its special commission, should and could appropriate the characteristics, the task, and the dignity of the State, thus itself becoming an organ of the State. (Barmen 1934: para. 5, quoted in Matheson, 1981)

Nazism, Barmen declares, must be rejected because it is idolatry. And with this rejection there went a repudiation of the Lutheran two-kingdoms doctrine which had led to a formal recognition of the autonomy of the secular sphere, and in practice to a systematic collusion between the main body of the German Church and the Nazi movement, a disastrous confusion of the swastika and the cross. The principal rejoinder to *The Barmen Declaration*, the *Ansbach Recommendation* formulated by Erlangen theologians, is a striking example of how those who proclaim the independence of the secular from theological scrutiny can land in a fatal collusion with monstrous immorality:

The law . . . binds each one of us to the estate into which we have been called by God and obligates us to the natural orders to which we are subject, such as family, nation, race (i.e. blood ties) . . . Since, moreover, God's will is always concerned with our here and now, it also binds us to the definite historical moment of our family, nation, race, i.e. to a specific moment in their history . . . Recognizing this, as faithful Christians we thank the Lord God for bestowing on our nation in its time of need the leader, Adolf Hitler, to be its 'pious and faithful governor' and for his desire to grant us a regime of 'discipline and honour' in the form of the National Socialist State. We therefore acknowledge our responsibility in God's sight to support the Leader's work in our respective callings and professions. (in Duchrow 1987: 12)

The supreme sadness about this controversy, however, is that the Nazis' behaviour towards the Jews nowhere appears. Barmen rang the alarm bells about Hitler's pretensions and rejected Nazi interference in the inner life of the church. This assertion of the freedom of the church and the direct challenge to Nazi claims and Nazi ideology were in the context extraordinarily courageous and perceptive. This makes it all the more painful that it was only isolated leaders such as Bonhoeffer and, somewhat later, Barth who identified the Jews and the death camps as *the* central issue which Christians must confront.

Later, in the 1950s and 1960s, there emerged a recognition that the issue of apartheid also was not simply a matter of ethics, but was a strictly theological issue which called for a direct theological response. In 1968 *A Message to the People of South Africa* was produced by the Joint Theological Commission of the South African Council of Churches and the South African Catholic Bishops' Conference. This suggested that it is impossible to witness to the truth of the gospel without denouncing false gospels. The system of apartheid, it argued, has become precisely this:

. . . This doctrine is being seen by many not merely as a temporary political policy but as a necessary and permanent expression of the will of God, and as the genuine form of Christian obedience for this country. But this doctrine, together with the hardships which are deriving from its implementation, forms a programme which is truly hostile to Christianity and can serve only to keep people away from the true knowledge of Christ.

There are alarming signs that this doctrine of separation has become, for many, a false faith, a novel Gospel which offers happiness and peace for the community and the individual. It holds out to men a security built not on Christ but on the theory of separation and the preservation of their racial identity. It presents separate development of our race-groups as a way for the people of South Africa to save themselves. Such a claim inevitably conflicts with the Christian Gospel, which offers salvation, both social and individual, through faith in Christ alone. (in de Gruchy and Villa-Vicencio 1983: 155)

In course of time this *Message* was followed by the Lutheran World Federation, the World Council of Churches, and the World Alliance of Reformed Churches all declaring apartheid to be sinful, and those defending it to be in a state of heresy. And, most significantly of all, the Dutch Reformed Mission Church, the 'coloured' daughter Church of the Dutch Reformed Church, produced in 1982 a *Confession* which derives conclusions from a careful doctrinal statement:

Therefore, we reject any doctrine which, in such a situation, sanctions in the name of the gospel or of the will of God the forced separation of people on the grounds of race and colour and thereby in advance obstructs and weakens the ministry and experience of reconciliation in Christ . . . We reject any ideology which would legitimate forms of injustice and any doctrine which is unwilling to resist such an ideology in the name of the gospel. (Cloete and Smit 1984: 3–4)

In the last decade or so there has been a widespread feeling in ecumenical circles that a similar confessional approach should be taken on a number of other issues. For instance, it has been suggested that there is now enough of a consensus among Christians about the incompatibility of waging nuclear war and the Christian faith to make this a confessional matter (the question of nuclear *deterrence* is still an issue on which

Christian opinion is so sharply divided that there is probably not the basis as yet for asserting that the rejection of nuclear deterrence is a clear implication of the Christian faith).

Ulrich Duchrow has recently raised the possibility of the world economic system becoming a confessional issue. He poses the question thus: 'If the service of Christ in the persons of his needy, poor and oppressed brothers and sisters is part of the very essence of the sacramental body of Christ, has the time come when the church, faced with the manifest failure of the economic institutions, must in obedience to its faith "put a spoke in the wheel"?' (Duchrow 1987: 59) The problem is, of course, complicated by the fact that the church is 'divided among active thieves, passive profiteers, and deprived victims' (p. 48). To pin-point the issue he continues,

Do thieves, profiteers and the victims of their depradations, all of whom call themselves Christians, continue to share together in the eucharist even if the thieves blatantly go on thieving and profiteering and disguising or denying its reality and extent? A Barmen-style theological declaration in a Western industrial society would need to deal explicitly with this guilt and offer encouragement and practical guidance for conversion'. (p. 111)

The rich, in other words, and all who benefit from the system at the expense of the poor, need to repent and change their ways or risk exclusion from the church.

In an important challenge to Duchrow's proposal, Professor Ronald Preston questions how useful a confessional repudiation of the world economic system such as Duchrow advocates would be. It would, Preston correctly argues, give no guidance whatever in dealing with the actual choices faced by people in the economic sphere. It reduces, he believes, a complex situation to simple black-and-white terms. Because Duchrow is an amateur in economics, Preston suggests, his whole discussion is based on a moral assessment of a series of extraordinarily broad and often suspect generalizations about the working of the economy (Preston 1988: 279–86).

It is easy to have sympathies both with Duchrow and with Preston. Duchrow reminds us that the moral and theological issues arising in a complex system are often amazingly simple, and we must not lose sight of this in a mass of technical analysis. Architects, chemists, transport economists, and many other academic specialists must have been involved in the construction and running of Hitler's extermination camps. One wonders how many of them recognized the appalling iniquity of the project in which they were involved. Systems and ideologies such as Nazism and apartheid do not only raise moral issues; they pose a direct challenge to the integrity of the Christian gospel, and therefore must be denounced and renounced if the good news of God's deliverance in Jesus Christ is to be announced. The question is a theological or confessional one. But Preston is right in suggesting that in many situations what Christians need is guidance, encouragement, and forgiveness in running systems and working within structures which, although far from ideal, are not as flagrantly wrong and evil as Nazism and apartheid, and need the leavening of Christian insight. The risk with this position is collusion with systems as they develop idolatrous pretensions and proclaim false gospels. The need is for sensitivity to discern the point at which a confessional stand requires to be made.

There is certainly an important place for occasional and emphatically confessional statements. What we are suggesting, however, is that there is a more general sense in which theology's contribution in the public realm must be confessional. Theology must speak from the heart of Christian belief, or hold its tongue. If theology finds nothing to say, no word, that is, that is rooted in the gospel, it is best to keep silence. But there is today an extraordinary openness and eagerness for something distinctive, for some constructive word which gives a clue to what is going on and puts things in the right perspective, for a truly prophetic theology. People in all sorts of corners of this strange land are straining to hear the skylark's song.

The Church in the Strange Land

The church is called to sing the songs of Zion in a strange land. But unlike those who sat down and wept by the waters of Babylon, we have to come to terms with the fact that as the church of Jesus Christ we are not, despite appearances, 'at home'. We are exiles and pilgrims, people who do not belong here, but who seek their true homeland, the city whose builder and maker is God. As we analyse with honesty the contemporary situation of the church in our strange land we find that the church now commands the allegiance of a minority—quite a small minority—of the population. Its power and influence are far less than once they were. The church and the Christian faith are increasingly pushed to the margins of things. Developments such as these are not to be welcomed; in many cases they should surely be resisted. But we must face realistically what is happening, and what has been happening for a considerable time. And we should recognize that these developments, threatening as they are to our inherited notions of what it means to be the church, are also bearers of possibilities of church renewal, of a recovery of an authentic understanding of what it means to be the church. Contemporary thinkers as varied as Karl Rahner, Leonardo Boff, and Alasdair MacIntyre all see new opportunities for a minority church, relatively powerless and operating more at the margins of things than at the centre. In the terms used by Dietrich Bonhoeffer there is the problem of the 'place' of the church: 'having lost its specific place, the Church is now only to be found in privileged places in the world . . . It has lost the yardstick for its *proper* place'. What is this 'proper place'? Bonhoeffer asserts that

No one knows in advance where this place, this centre, will be. Historically speaking, it may be right on the fringe, as was Galilee in the Roman Empire or Wittenberg in the 16th century. But God will make this place visible and everyone then has to include it in his itinerary. All that the Church can do is to attest the centre of the world which God alone decides. It must try to make space for God's work'. (in Duchrow 1987: 22)

Three ways of 'making space' are of particular relevance to our theme:

(*a*) The church, that means each congregation, may be an experiment in fellowship, in living together in love and truth. Just as the Christian church refreshed a tired and jaded classical social theory by providing models of fellowship and love (Wolin 1961: 96), so in our 'strange land' there is need for exemplifications and experiments in fellowship. Before the church may address the world she must demonstrate that she takes the message seriously herself, like Chaucer's poor parson:

> Christ's lore and his Apostles twelve
> He taught—and first he followed it himself.

Such experiments, such fellowships, are important as signs and gestures, as little manifestations of the Kingdom, as ways of affirming worth and dignity, as expressions of solidarity with those who are already poor or marginalized, as exemplifications of the authenticity of the message.

(*b*) The church needs to rediscover itself as a forum for moral discourse. The day of pre-packaged answers and 'moral instruction' is long past. We now realize more fully than in the past the increasing complexity of many modern ethical dilemmas, and hence the impossibility of simple, rule-of-thumb solutions. This, according to Karl Rahner, has an important consequence for Christian moral teaching:

Consciences must be formed, not primarily by way of casuistic instruction, going into more and more concrete details, but by being roused and trained for autonomous and responsible decisions in the concrete, complex situations of human life which are no longer completely soluble down to the last detail, in fields never considered by the older morality, precisely because they were then unknown and even now cannot be adequately mastered by a rational casuistry (Rahner 1974: 68).

The kind of prolonged, open, participative, and frank engagement with great questions which we found pioneered by the US Catholic bishops in the formulation of their two pastoral letters represents a fascinating insight into the possibilities. A new kind and a new quality of reflection on public policy is becoming possible in churches which are realistic about their own situations, theologically serious, cogent in argumentation, attentive to the facts, and willing to pioneer.

(*c*) The new marginality of the churches is widely experienced as threatening by Christians. It is indeed a new situation for those who have been accustomed to the comforting vestiges of Christendom. Yet one may interpret the margin in the light of passages such as Hebrews 13 as the place where Jesus suffered, outside the camp, for the sake of the life of the city; the place of discernment and of redemption, the place to which Christians are called to keep company with their Lord: 'Let us therefore go forth to him outside the camp, bearing abuse for him.'

And let there be no mistake about this: innovations, new ways of looking at things, fresh insights tend to come from the margins. Surprisingly, even Bryan Wilson, a sociologist of religion who has sometimes given the impression of dancing on the grave of religious faith, in the conclusion of his *Religion in a Sociological Perspective*, sees the necessary refreshment of the social order emerging from the religion of the margins:

It does not appear that men will be able to remake the world we have lost, and unless there is a massive change of heart, a veritable revolution of many of the conveniences of modern life and organization, it is difficult to see how the otherwise irrevocable pattern of societal order could be reinfused with religious inspiration. As yet, only at the margins and in the interstices, and principally in the domain of private life, has such religious endeavour been effective in allowing some men, at least, to transcend the present discontents, and in producing, by way of the dissemination of dispositions of goodwill and commitment, that salt of the earth that is necessary to maintain the social order. (Wilson 1982: 175)

Being at the margin presents new opportunities and new responsibilities for Christians and for Churches concerned for the flourishing of women and men at the centre of things, in the camp, in the city as well as at the margins.

Mystique and Politique

'Everything starts with mystique and ends with politique', declared that strange, profound thinker, Charles Péguy. His epigram is, of course, ambiguous. It may be read as meaning that mystique tends to degenerate into politique, or, conversely, that mystique finds its goal and fulfilment in politique. But what is certain is that for Péguy the two must be related, and the proper relationship is a subtle and delicate matter.

Mystique is something that calls for unconditional loyalty, that makes totalitarian claims, that speaks of the ultimate and the transcendent. The mystique is a mystery to be loved and adored, explored and lived, rather than a problem to be resolved or a puzzle to be unravelled. Theology's role is to be the guardian, critic, and expounder of this mystique; and theology's perennial temptation is to resolve the mystique into something simple, even banal, which does not engage with the profundities of life but only with comparatively superficial issues.

Politique, on the other hand, for Péguy is essential for human flourishing. It has accordingly an immense dignity and importance. But politique deals in relativities and compromises; it chooses between evils rather than realizing an absolute and unconditional good. The ultimate issues of life are inaccessible to it. Politique involves the prudent balancing of interests and claims, the maintenance of a relative peace, and the constant struggle to achieve a tolerable approximation to justice. Mystique is the lark's song, the Lord's song in a strange land. It speaks of the New Jerusalem, the polity which politique can never build, in which unity and harmony and an undisturbed fellowship with God will be the basis for true peace and justice.

Péguy was well aware of the danger of 'the degradation of a mystique into a politique', and knew that 'the mystique should not be devoured by the politique to which it gave birth' (Péguy 1958: 31). The mystique cannot be resolved without remainder into a politique; it is more than, and other than, a politique, even if it has a necessary relation to politique.

Following Péguy, we suggest that the mystique nourishes the politique: 'Mysticism may be the laughing stock of politics but all the same, it is the mystic who nourishes politics' (Péguy 1958: 48). And the mystic nourishes politics in particularly important ways today: in questioning assumptions and generating fresh priorities. The US Roman Catholic Bishops, for instance, cut through the hard shell of economic debate to assert the kernel of the matter: 'The fundamental moral criterion for all economic decisions, policies and institutions is this: they must be at the service of *all people*, especially the poor' (US Catholic Bishops 1986: par. 28). And, 'The dignity of the human person, realised in community with others, is the criterion against which all aspects of economic life must be measured' (US Catholic Bishops 1986: par. 28). This affirmation that the economic system is for the sake of human flourishing, and that true prosperity is impossible without a special concern for the poor and the excluded runs strongly counter to much influential economic and political thinking today, both of the right and of the left. Again, it is significant how through reports such as *Not Just for the Poor* (1987), *Faith in the City* (1985), and *Just Sharing* (1988) the British Churches are exploring and reaffirming the priority of fellowship and the nature of *koinonia* in opposition to the confident and seductive theories of possessive individualism on the one hand, and a callous collectivism on the other. One hopes that this may provide the basis for a renewal of politically and economically viable notions of fellowship.

Similarly, theology and the churches are exploring and reaffirming ideas of justice derived from the Bible and the Christian tradition. This is particularly important at a time when influential social theorists such as Friedrich von Hayek proclaim social justice to be a 'mirage', and the establishment and maintenance of social and distributive justice to be no proper part of government's responsibility. Such thinkers redefine justice in such a way that they can declare that injustice cannot result from the transactions of the market, because the adverse results of the market are unintended. The poor and the weak have no claim on government or the community; anything that is done for them is out of pure generosity (Hayek, 1976; Joseph and Sumption 1979). This position is developed further by Robert Nozick, who defines justice in purely procedural terms. For him there is no such thing as distributive or social justice. Individuals are entitled to gain as much for themselves as they can, provided they follow 'fair' procedures, and have no obligations towards their neighbours. Furthermore, government is not entitled to intervene to redistribute resources or establish social justice. It simply has the responsibility of ensuring 'due process' in the courts, and correct procedures in the market (Nozick 1974). The alternative utilitarian view derives justice from social utility: justice is the greatest good of the greatest number. Here a widening gap between the prosperous and the disadvantaged is not itself a problem provided the aggregate of social benefit is increased. There is here no 'preferential option for the poor', and in this respect there appears to be a sharp divergence from biblical understandings of justice. John Rawls's immensely influential *A Theory of Justice* (1973) gives more attention to the disadvantaged, but has been criticized for treating inequality too lightly. Furthermore, there is apparently no way, as Alasdair MacIntyre has pointed out, of arbitrating between such competing notions of justice, which all claim to rest on purely rational foundations, in the absence of an agreed criterion (MacIntyre 1981).

It is not a little encouraging that today theologians who believe that contemporary philosophical accounts of justice are inadequate theologically, are seeking afresh a Christian approach which has a distinctive character, is founded on the biblical witness, and may provide a more satisfactory foundation for a theory of justice. Such Christian explorations of justice always relate justice and community very closely. Hence they are primarily accounts of social and distributive justice. Alastair Campbell, for instance, sees the view that the material world is the inalienable property of human beings, who are themselves wholly autonomous agents with no obligations beyond defence against infringements of personal liberty, as 'simply incompatible with Christian beliefs in God as creator, as a covenant God and as a God of reconciling love. These basic beliefs', he continues,

require that justice and injustice must always be seen in terms of respect for God's creation, responsibility for our community and love of neighbour, whether near or distant . . . Material prosperity, individual choice and the possession of private property are not ultimate goals in a Christian scale of values: each must serve the end of love, through the enhancement of the whole community (with special attention to its vulnerable members) and through a concern and respect for all of nature. Those with power over people and material things are merely 'stewards', answerable for the good or evil which may come from their treatment of God's creatures . . . A society like ours which tolerates increasing child poverty and inadequate facilities for the frail and handicapped is becoming like a society which tolerates falsehood—it will eventually lose all sense of the meaning and worth of the non-material, allowing health and truth to become merely aspects of the individual's advantage over others. (Campbell 1988: 28)

In all these ways, and many others, mystique nourishes politics today; it also sustains vision and hope in times of cynicism, despair, and hopelessness.

How can we sing the Lord's song in an increasingly strange land? Only by remembering Zion, by attending to the skylark's song, by labouring at application and translation, aware always of the limits of our efforts and the dangers of distortion. The lark continues to swoop down into the well to make us frogs restless and delighted with its sweet song. And that, ultimately, is our assurance that grace, mercy, and justice have the last word, and that truth will triumph over falsehood.

REFERENCES

ABRAMS, M., GERARD, D., and TIMMS, N., eds. (1985), *Values and Social Change in Britain*, London.

Archbishop of Canterbury's Commission on Urban Priority Areas (1985), *Faith in the City: A Call for Action by Church and Nation*, London.

BAGEHOT, W. (1888), *The English Constitution*, 5th edn., London.

BARTH, K. (1939), *Church and State*, London.

——(1969), *Church Dogmatics* I/I, Edinburgh.

BCC (British Council of Churches) (1982), *Poverty* (Papers written by a working party of the Division of Community Affairs), London.

BENNETT, J. C. (1954), *Christian Social Action*, London.

BERGER, P. (1970), *A Rumour of Angels*, London.

BERKHOF, H. (1953, ET1962), *Christ and the Powers*, trans. J. H. Yoder, Scottdale, Pennsylvania.

BIGGAR, N. (1987), 'Any News of What's Good for Society?' *Latimer Comment* 24, Oxford.

——(1988), *Theological Politics: A Critique of 'Faith in the City'*, Oxford.

BONHOEFFER, D. (1954), *Life Together*, London.

BSR (Church of England Board for Social Responsibility) (1966), *Putting Asunder: A Divorce Law for Contemporary Society*, London.

——(1982), *The Church and the Bomb: Nuclear Weapons and Christian Conscience*, London.

——(1984), *Perspectives on Economics: Reflections on Aspects of the Changing British Economic System*, London.

——(1987a), *Changing Britain: Social Diversity and Moral Unity*, London.

——(1987b), *Not Just For the Poor*, London.

CAIRD, G. B. (1956), *Principalities and Powers*, Oxford.

CAMPBELL, A. V. (1978), *Medicine, Health and Justice*, Edinburgh.

——(1988), 'Health, Justice and Community: A Theological View', *Inequalities in Health in the 1980s*, CTPI Occasional Paper Number 13, Edinburgh.

CARR, W. (1981), *Angels and Principalities*, Cambridge.

CHESTERTON, G. K. (1911), *Heretics*, London.

CLOETE, G. D. and SMIT, D. J., eds. (1984), *A Moment of Truth: The Confession of the Dutch Reformed Mission Church 1982*, Grand Rapids.

Crowther–Kilbrandon Commission (1969), *Commission on the Constitution: Minutes of Evidence II; Scotland*, London.

CULLMANN, O. (1951), *Christ and Time*, London.

—— (1957), *The State in the New Testament*, London.

DAVIS, C. (1980), *Theology and Political Society*, Cambridge.

DIBELIUS, M. (1909), *Die Geisterwelt im Glauben des Paulus*, Göttingen.

DONNE, J. (1945), *Devotions XVII*, in John Donne, *Complete Poems and Selected Prose*, London.

DUCHROW, U. (1987), *Global Economy: A Confessional Issue for the Churches?*, Geneva.

DUFF, E. (1956), *The Social Thought of the World Council of Churches*, London.

DUNSTAN, G. R. (1974), *The Artifice of Ethics*, London.

—— (1982), 'Theological Method in the Deterrence Debate', in G. Goodwin, ed., *Ethics and Nuclear Deterrence*, London.

EDWARDS, D. L. (1973), *The British Churches Turn to the Future*, London.

ELLIOT, A. and FORRESTER, D. B., eds. (1986), *The Scottish Churches and the Political Process Today*, Edinburgh.

ELLIOTT, C. (1978), Vision and Utopia, *Theology*, 172–9.

—— (1987), *Comfortable Compassion? Poverty, Power and the Church*, London.

EVERLING, O. (1888), *Die paulinische Angelologie und Dämonologie*, Göttingen.

FIELD, F. (1985), *The Politics of Paradise*, London.

FORRESTER, D. B. (1986), 'The Theological Task', In H. Davis, ed., *Ethics and Defence: Power and Responsibility in the Nuclear Age*, Oxford.

—— and SKENE, D., eds. (1988), *Just Sharing: A Christian Approach to the Distribution of Wealth, Income and Benefits*, London.

GEORGE, S. (1988), *A Fate Worse than Debt*, Harmondsworth.

GIDDENS, A. (1987), *Social Theory and Modern Sociology*, Oxford.

GILL, R. (1988), *Beyond Decline: A Challenge to the Churches*, London.

GILBERT, A. D. (1980), *The Making of Post-Christian Britain: A history of the Secularization of Modern Society*, Harlow.

GRUCHY, J. de and VILLA-VICENCIO, C., eds. (1983), *Apartheid is a Heresy*, Cape Town.

HABGOOD, J. (1983), *Church and Nation in a Secular Age*, London.

HARNACK, A. von (1904–5), *The Expansion of Christianity in the First Three Centuries*, 2 vols., London.

HASTINGS, A. (1986), *A History of English Christianity 1920–1985*, London.

HAUERWAS, S. (1983), *The Peaceable Kingdom—A Primer in Christian Ethics*, London.

HAYEK, F. A. (1976), *The Mirage of Social Justice*, London.

HOLLOWAY, D. (1987), *A Nation under God*, Eastbourne.

IGNATIEFF, M. (1984), *The Needs of Strangers*, London.

JOSEPH, K. and SUMPTION, J. (1979), *Equality*, London.

Kairos Document (1986), London.

KUITERT, H. M. (1986), *Everything is Politics but Politics is not Everything: A Theological Perspective on Faith and Politics*, London.

LANE, C. (1981), *The Rites of Rulers: Ritual in Industrial Society —The Soviet Case*, Cambridge.

LASSWELL, H. D. (1958), *Politics—Who Gets What, When, How*, New York.

LEBACQZ, K. (1986*a*), *The Three 'R's' of Justice*, Oxford.

—— (1986*b*), *Six Theories of Justice*, Minneapolis.

—— (1987), *Justice in an Unjust World—Foundations for a Christian Approach to Justice*, Minneapolis.

McCANN, D. (1981), 'A Second Look at Middle Axioms', *The Annual of the Society of Christian Ethics*, Dallas.

McCLENDON, J. W. Jun. (1986), *Ethics—Systematic Theology*, i, Nashville.

MACGREGOR, G. H. C. (1954), 'Principalities and Powers: The Cosmic Background of St Paul's Thought', *New Testament Studies*, 1, 17–28.

MACINTYRE, A. (1956), 'A Society without a Metaphysics', *The Listener*; 13 Sept., 375–6.

—— (1967), *Secularization and Moral Change*, London.

MacIntyre, A. (1981), *After Virtue: A Study in Moral Theory*, London.

—— (1988), *Whose Justice? Which Rationality?*, London.

Mackenzie, N., ed. (1958), *Conviction*, London.

Macmurray, J. (1961), *Persons in Relation*, London.

Mahoney, J. (1987), *The Making of Moral Theology: A Study of the Roman Catholic Tradition*, Oxford.

Matheson, P., ed. (1981), *The Third Reich and the Christian Churches*, Edinburgh.

Metz, J. B. (1980), *Faith in History and Society*, London.

Morrison, C. D. (1960), *The Powers That Be*, London.

Moyser, G., ed. (1985), *Church and Politics Today: The Role of the Church of England in Contemporary Politics*, Edinburgh.

Muir, E. (1960), *Collected Poems*, London.

Neuhaus, R. J. (1984), *The Naked Public Square: Religion and Democracy in America*, Grand Rapids.

Newbigin, L. (1981), 'Politics and the Covenant', *Theology*, 84/701, 356–63.

—— (1983), *The Other Side of 84: Questions for the Churches*, London.

—— (1986), *Foolishness to the Greeks: The Gospel and Western Culture*, London.

Niebuhr, R. (1944), *The Nature and Destiny of Man*, 2 vols., London.

Norman, E. R. (1979), *Christianity and the World Order*, Oxford.

Nozick, R. (1974), *Anarchy, State and Utopia*, Oxford.

O'Donovan, O. (1986), *Resurrection and Moral Order*, Leicester.

Oestreicher, P. (1986), *The Double Cross*, London.

Oldham, J. H., and t'Hooft, V. (1937), *The Church and its Function in Society*, London.

Péguy, C. (1958), *Temporal and Eternal*, London.

Preston, R. H. (1981), *Explorations in Theology*, 8, London.

—— (1983), *Church and Society in the Late Twentieth Century: The Economic and Political Task*, London.

—— (1988), 'Christian Faith and Capitalism', *The Ecumenical Review* 40/2, 279–86.

Rahner, K. (1974), *The Shape of the Church to Come*, London.

Ramsey, P. (1968), *The Just War*, New York.

—— (1969), *Who Speaks for the Church? A Critique of the 1966 Geneva Conference on Church and Society*, Edinburgh.

RAWLS, J. (1973), *A Theory of Justice*, Oxford.

ROSZAK, T. (1970), *The Making of a Counter Culture*, London.

RUBENSTEIN, R. L., and ROTH, J. K. (1987), *Approaches to Auschwitz*, London.

SCRUTON, R. (1980), *The Meaning of Conservatism*, Harmondsworth.

SOLZHENITSYN, A. (1971), *Cancer Ward*, Harmondsworth.

STEWART, J. S. (1951), 'On a Neglected Emphasis in New Testament Theology', *Scottish Journal of Theology* 4, 292–301.

SUGGATE, A. (1987), *William Temple and Christian Social Ethics Today*, Edinburgh.

TAWNEY, R. H. (1921), *The Acquisitive Society*, London.

—— (1926), *Religion and the Rise of Capitalism*, London.

—— (1931), *Equality*, London.

—— (1953), *The Attack and Other Papers*, London.

—— (1972), *R. H. Tawney's Commonplace Book*, ed. J. M. Winter and D. M. Joslin, Cambridge.

TAYLOR, M. H., ed. (1982), *Christians and the Future of Social Democracy*, Ormskirk and Northridge.

TEMPLE, W. (1942), *Christianity and Social Order*, Harmondsworth.

T'HOOFT, V. (1948), *The Lordship of Christ*, London.

TINKER, H. (1979), *The Ordeal of Love: C. F. Andrews and India*, Delhi.

US Catholic Bishops (1983), 'The Challenge of Peace: God's Promise and Our Response. A Pastoral Letter on War and Peace', Origins, 13/1, 19 May. Also published in 1983 in book form by CTS/SPCK.

—— (1986), 'Economic Justice for All: Catholic Social Teaching and the US Economy' (Third Draft), *Origins*, 16/3, 5 June.

VILLA-VICENCIO, C. (1986), *Between Christ and Caesar. Classic and Contemporary Texts on Church and State*, Cape Town.

WALLIS, J. (1983), *The New Radical*, Tring.

WEBER, M. (1958), *The Religion of India: The Sociology of Hinduism and Buddhism*, New York.

WEST, P. (1986), 'A Christian Approach to the Problem of Security? A Reply to Gordon Dunstan', *Kings Theological Review*, 5/2, 55–8.

WILLIAMS, J. A. (1985), '"A Bishop Should Speak Out" But What Can He Say? Secularisation, Establishment and the Voice of the Church', *Crucible* Jan.–Mar., 15–23.

WILSON, B. (1982), *Religion in Sociological Perspective*, Oxford.

WINK, W. (1984), *Naming the Powers: The Language of Power in the New Testament* (The Powers, i), Philadelphia.

——(1986), *Unmasking the Powers* (The Powers, ii), Philadelphia.

WOLIN, S. (1961), *Politics and Vision*, London.

WCC (World Council of Churches) (1948), *The Church and the Disorder of Society*, London.

INDEX